THE
HOLY BIBLE
AND
THE LAW

By

J. W. EHRLICH

OCEANA PUBLICATIONS, INC.

NEW YORK, N. Y.

But as for thee, stand thou here by me, and I will speak unto
thee all the commandments, . . . which thou shalt teach them,
that they may do them. . . .

Deuteronomy 5:31

PURPOSE

THE HOLY BIBLE AND THE LAW is intended as a quick-finder for the literate citizen, the student, the men of cloth, the lawyer, the social worker, the doctor, the judge, the orator, the law office, the library, and the teacher. Each legal subject has been, wherever possible, set out in plain, non-technical language, and the Holy Bible has been quoted without comment except citation to the source book. No distinction is made between the various and varied biblical translations, but all quotations are found in the Hebrew, Catholic and Protestant Bibles most commonly used today.

TABLE OF CONTENTS

INTRODUCTION

THE BIBLE (Greek-biblos, book) consists of sixty-six books aside from those of the Apocrypha. The word Bible was first applied to the Hebrew Scripture in the second century A.D. (Second Epistle to Corinth) and has been used for the combined Old and New Testaments since the fifth century A.D. The word Bible does not occur in the text of the Scriptures.

The so-called Books of Moses are also known as the Pentateuch (Greek, five scrolls), or the Law. Much of the Pentateuch goes back to the remote past, and other parts of it may have been written as late as the Fifth Century B.C. It came to be regarded as authoritative about 400 B.C.

It is impossible to determine exactly when the first collection of sacred books was made. It is uncertain at what date the Hebrews, under the leadership of Esdras, bound themselves to the observance of the Torah, or Law of Moses. From the prologue of Ecclesiasticus, it appears that a collection which included 'the Law, the Prophets, and the Writings' was in existence in 130 B.C. It is unknown by what authority it was determined which books should be included in the collection. In all probability the books were in the custody of the priesthood. It is reasonable to assume that the Scribes subsequently asserted their authority to exclude books from the collection. However, the vagueness of this determination is seen in the existence of two canons. The Palestinian canon, represented by the Old Testament in Hebrew, and the Alexandrine canon, represented by the Old Testament in

Greek, which contained books not admitted into the Palestinian collection.

These five books of Moses were the most highly venerated of the sacred books. Torah actually means 'instruction' or 'doctrine,' rather than 'law'; and a large portion of the books of Moses is narrative. From the narrative portions as well as from the legal portions were deduced conclusions about God, His providence, and human conduct. 'Law,' however, expresses accurately the attitude of the Hebrews toward these books. The basis of legal observance was faith in the covenant of God with Israel and in divine retribution.

The Law, however, was more than a series of regulations of external conduct. It was possible for Hillel to sum it up in the rule, 'Do not to another what you would not have him do to you,' and for Jesus to point out as its greatest and first commandment, 'Thou shalt love the Lord thy God with thy whole heart,' and as the second, 'Thou shalt love thy neighbor as thyself.'

Mosaic law was studied carefully for generations. Extensions and refinements in that law were made by scholars and orally transmitted to their students.

Many interpretations of the Bible developed, and in the Third Century A.D. these were codified in written form called the Mishnah. Later, scholars commented and elaborated upon the Mishnah and thus created a new work called the Gemara. Thus, the Mishnah and Gemara resulted in two compilations each known as the Talmud, one in Palestine in the Fourth Century; the other in Babylon in the Fifth.

The Talmud treats of civil and religious law, history, mathematics, astronomy, medicine, metaphysics, and theosophy. It passes from law to myth, from jest to earnest. It is replete with chaste diction, legendary illustration, touches of pathos, bursts of genuine eloquence, finished rhetoric, and flashes of wit and sarcasm.

By 200 A.D. the New Testament was generally accepted as Scripture. In 367 A.D. Athanasius, Bishop of Alexandria, in a public letter, listed the twenty-seven books which have been held as authoritative to this day.

The fourteen books of the Apocrypha (Greek, for "hidden" or "obscure") have not been included in the Protestant Bible since the beginning of the Ninteenth Century. There are editions of the Bible containing the Apocrypha, but since the books are rejected as non-inspired, although of Hebrew origin, most Hebrew and Protestant religious leaders have ignored their beauty and value. The Catholic Bible contains some of the Apocrypha.

Blackstone, in his commentaries on the Laws of England, wrote that Divine Providence has been pleased at sundry times and in divers manners to discover and enforce its laws by an immediate and direct revelation. And that the doctrines thus discovered are called the revealed or divine law, and are to be found only in the Holy Scriptures.

Mosaic law is a law of principles, directing man in the ways of righteousness, happiness and tranquility. The principles were not of immediate creation, but grew through thousands of years of human experience.

Research has established that much of the Five Books of Moses gradually built up during some eight or ten centuries of development. It is believed that Moses codified the laws which had long been known. In Genesis 26:5,

God said of Abraham that he "kept my charge, my commandments, my statutes, and my laws," which indicates that the laws of Moses must have been promulgated long before.

The translations and the various versions of the Bible are: 1. The "Septuagint," (seventy) so called because the translation from the Hebrew to the Greek language in 285 B.D. was allegedly made by seventy men. 2. The "Peshito" (literal) translation, embracing the Old and New Testaments was made about 200 A.D. for the Syrian Christians. 3. The "Vulgate" (vulgus—for the common people) translation of the Old and New Testament into Latin was made about 400 A.D. It is the standard Bible of the Roman Catholic Church. 4. The "King James Version" of the Holy Scriptures—the English translation—was first published in 1611.

In 1250 A.D. the Holy Scriptures were divided into chapters by Cardinal Hugo de Sancto Caro. The division into verses was made about 1550 A.D. The first versified New Testament in English was published in 1557, and in 1560 A.D. the entire Bible was printed in versified form.

It should be noted that in the versification there is much repetition as evidenced in the Seventh Chapter of Numbers which has 89 verses. Of these, verses 15, 21, 27, 33, 39, 45, 51, 57, 63, 69 and 75 are alike.

Verses 16, 22, 28, 34, 40, 46, 52, 58, 64, 70, 76 and 82 are the same.

Verses 26, 32, 38, 44, 50, 56, 62, 68, 74 and 80 are identical.

Verses 25, 37, 49, 61, 67, 73 and 98 are worded the same.

Verses 38 and 55 are alike.

Verse 43 differs from verses 31 and 55 in only one word: where verse 43 reads "a," verses 31 and 55 read "one."

The oldest available manuscripts of substantial parts of the Old Testament in Hebrew are dated 897 and 916 A.D. The oldest manuscript of the entire Old Testament in Hebrew is dated 1008 A.D. The oldest manuscript of the Bible in Greek is the Codex Vaticanus dated in the Fourth Century, a possession of the Vatican Library. The Septuagint Bible (Greek) is the version of the Bible most quoted in the New Testament.

Martin Luther translated the Bible into German in 1534 A.D.

At the end of the Fourteenth Century, John Wyclif made his translation of the Bible from Latin to English, and those who dared to read his work were persecuted. The English law in 1414 provided that those who read the Scriptures in English should "forfeit land, cattle, life and goods from their heirs forever." Some were burned at the stake for the offense, with copies of the Bible dangling from their necks.

For the English-speaking world, the name of William Tyndale is synonymous with the story of the Bible in English. Because of the prohibition against translating the Bible into language readable by the so-called average man, his work in translating the Bible from Hebrew and Greek made him a fugivitive from the England of Henry VIII. Hunted like a wild beast by the Inquisition, he was finally caught in 1536, was imprisoned, strangled, and burned at the stake in Velvorde, Belgium.

The Five Books of Moses contain all the law, and while the laws in Exodus presumably date from the 15th Century B.C., those in Deuteronomy probably were not proclaimed until about the 5th Century B.C. The best known are, of course, the Ten Commandments.

There are two versions of the Ten Commandments; one in Exodus, which is the most commonly accepted version, the other in Deuteronomy. It is assumed that both versions were in exsitence hundreds of years before the five Books of Moses were reduced to writing.

The Ten Commandments begin with the declaration that Israel's God brought him out of Egypt and bondage. Israel shall have no other gods, and shall not make any graven image or representation of anything as an idol to bow down to and serve. The sin of idolatry is proscribed by the admonition that God will punish the children for the sins of their fathers unto the third and fourth generation, and that God is merciful to those who love Him and keep His commandments. Next comes the prohibition against taking His name in vain, and is followed by the directive to keep the Sabbath holy as a rest day from all work for man, beast, and for the stranger. Honoring father and mother is the next commandment. Forbidden are murder, adultery, theft, and false testimony. The Commandments conclude with a prohibition of covetousness of anything belonging to one's neighbor.

The differences in the two versions of the Commandments form an interesting study. While there is no essential variation so far as vital obligations are concerned, verbal changes occur, and in one instance, that of the Sabbath, an entirely different reason is adduced for its observance. The slight variants in the Masoretic text, occasional differences in words, as for instance "covet" for "desire," "Remember the Sabbath," in one case, and "Keep" in the other, and "false witness" in one, and "a witness of deceit" in the other; some additions and amplifications, all this is sought to be explained as due to carelessness on the part of the transcribers. But the variation in the reason alleged for the Sabbath cannot be so readily explained. The Exodus Version connects it with creation; that of Deuteronomy associates it with Israel's release from Egyptian slavery.

The division of the Ten Commandments is another matter of inquiry. As it was written on two tablets of stone and on both sides, its arrangement would have been naturally one group of five "words," each on one stone. So, in fact, is the statement as to the original division made by Josephus ('Antiquitates' Vol. III, 5, 4) and by Phil ('De Decalogo' 12) the first group of five, including the commandments referring to our conduct toward our neighbors.

Another variation is the sequence of certain of the "words" which differ in various versions. The Masoretic text, Josephus, the Syrian Hexapla agree as to the order of the prohibitions against murder, adultery, and theft, but the Septuagint, Codex Alexandrinus and Abrosianus have the sequence of "murder, theft and adultery," while Philo ('De Decalogo' 12) the first group of five, including Codex Vaticanus "adultery, theft, murder"—slight variations, it is true; but in so fundamental a code as the Commandments one would expect uniformity throughout. No less peculiar is the diversity in the numbering of the different commandments.

According to the Jewish tradition, Ex 20:2, forms the first, while Verses 3-6, constitute the second. The Codex Vaticanus of the Septuagint and the Deuteronomy of Ambrosianus have a similar arrangement. Josephus and Philo regard Verse 3 as first, Verses 4-6 as second, Verse 7 as third, Verses 8-11 as fourth, Verse 12 as fifth, Verse 13 as sixth, Verse 14 as seventh, Verse 15 as eighth, Verse 16 as ninth, and Verse 17 as the tenth Commandment. The Roman Catholic and Lutheran combine Verses 3-6 into the first, and every commandment is advanced by one to the last, the traditional Jewish "tenth" being divided into ninth and tenth, to maintain the traditional number.

Most view the Ten Commandments solely as religious rules, but our courts have predicated decisions on much that is in the Bible. In 1899, the West Virginia Supreme Court said: "These Commandments, which, like a collection of diamonds, bear testimony to their own intrinsic worth, in themselves appeal to us as coming from a super-human or divine source, and no conscientious or reasonable man has yet been able to find a flaw in them. Absolutely flawless, negative in terms, but positive in meaning, they easily stand at the head of our whole moral system, and no nation or people can long continue a happy existence in open violation of them."

Law, generally, is defined as a rule of human action or conduct. Laws are meant to regulate and direct the acts and rights of man. Every man belongs to himself, and has the right to do as he pleases with himself so long as he accords the same right to others, and, further, that he does not do unto others what he would not have them do unto him. This principle is the foundation of English and American law. The Bible embodies these fundamentals which have attained legal effectiveness among nearly all peoples. Much of the law of England and America is founded upon Mosaic Law.

Without law, man would be plunged back into the chaos from which he emerged at the dawn of civilization. Law creates an orderly society, where mankind may follow his pursuits, secure in the knowledge that his rights will be protected and his obligations enforced. The law is so powerful that it is the only protection the individual has against the tyranny of his government. Man searching for the foundation of our law can find no firmer ground than the Bible.

No attempt is made herein to explain every refinement and technicality of our present laws. Enough is stated in general to give the reader a base for comparison of today's law with that in the Bible, though thousands of years separate the two.

Different? We will see.

San Francisco, California, 1961.   J. W. EHRLICH

CONTENTS AND ORDER OF THE BOOKS

OF

THE HOLY SCRIPTURES (Hebrew)

The Masoretic Text

Genesis
Exodus
Leviticus
Numbers
Deuteronomy
Joshua
Judges
1 Samuel
2 Samuel
1 Kings
2 Kings
Isaiah
Jeremiah
Ezekiel
Hosea
Joel
Amos
Obadiah
Jonah
Micah

Nahum
Habakkuk
Zephaniah
Haggai
Zechariah
Malachi
Psalms
Proverbs
Job
Song of Songs
Ruth
Lamentations
Ecclesiastes
Esther
Daniel
Ezra
Nehemiah
1 Chronicles
2 Chronicles

CONTENTS AND ORDER OF THE BOOKS

OF

THE KING JAMES VERSION

(Protestant)

THE OLD TESTAMENT

Genesis	2 Chronicles	Daniel
Exodus	Ezra	Hosea
Leviticus	Nehemiah	Joel
Numbers	Esther	Amos
Deuteronomy	Job	Obadiah
Joshua	Psalms	Jonah
Judges	Proverbs	Micah
Ruth	Ecclesiastes	Nahum
1 Samuel	The Song of Solomon	Habakkuk
2 Samuel	Isaiah	Zephaniah
1 Kings	Jeremiah	Haggai
2 Kings	Lamentations	Zechariah
1 Chronicles	Ezekiel	Malachi

THE NEW TESTAMENT

Matthew	Ephesians	To the Hebrews
Mark	Philippians	James
Luke	Colossians	1 Peter
John	1 Thessalonians	2 Peter
The Acts	2 Thessalonians	1 John
Romans	1 Timothy	2 John
1 Corinthians	2 Timothy	3 John
2 Corinthians	Titus	Jude
Galatians	Philemon	Revelation

CONTENTS AND ORDER OF THE BOOKS
OF
THE DOUAY VERSION
(Catholic)

THE OLD TESTAMENT

Genesis

Exodus

Leviticus

Numbers

Deuteronomy

Josue (Joshua)

Judges

Ruth

1 Kings (1 Samuel)

2 Kings (2 Samuel)

3 Kings (1 Kings)

4 Kings (2 Kings)

1 Paralipomenon (1 Chronicles)

2 Paralipomenon (2 Chronicles)

1 Esdras (Ezra)

2 Esdras (Nehemiah)

Tobias (Tobit)

Judith

Esther

Job

Psalms

Proverbs

Ecclesiastes

Canticle of Canticles (Song of Solomon)

Wisdom

Ecclesiasticus

Isaias (Isaiah)

Jeremias (Jeremiah)

Lamentations

Baruch

Ezechiel (Ezekiel)

Daniel

Osee (Hosea)

Joel

Amos

Abdias (Obadiah)

Jonas (Jonah)

Micheas (Micah)

Nahum

Habacuc (Habakkuk)

Sophonias (Zephaniah)

Aggeus (Haggai)

Zacharias (Zechariah)

Malachias (Malachi)

1 Machabees

2 Machabees

THE NEW TESTAMENT

St. Matthew

St. Mark

St. Luke

St. John

The Acts of the Apostles

St. Paul to the Romans

1 Corinthians

2 Corinthians

Galatians

Ephesians

Philippians

Colossians

1 Thessalonians

2 Thessalonians

1 Timothy

2 Timothy

Titus

Philemon

To the Hebrews

The Epistle of St. James

1 St. Peter

2 St. Peter

1 St. John

2 St. John

3 St. John

St. Jude

The Apocalypse of St. John
    the Apostle (Revelation)

CONTENTS AND ORDER OF THE BOOKS

OF

THE APOCRYPHA

THE TEN COMMANDMENTS

A COMPARISON

THE FIRST COMMANDMENT

HEBREW VERSION
I am the Lord thy God, who brought thee out of the land of Egypt, out of the house of bondage.

CATHOLIC VERSION
I am the Lord thy God. Thou shalt not have strange Gods before me.

PROTESTANT VERSION
I am the Lord thy God. Thou shalt have no other Gods before me.

THE SECOND COMMANDMENT

Thou shalt have no other Gods before me. Thou shalt not make unto thee a graven image, not any manner of likeness, of any thing that is in heaven above, or that is in the earth beneath, or that is in the water under the earth; Thou shalt not bow down unto them, nor serve them; for I the Lord thy God am a jealous God, visiting the iniquity of the fathers upon the children unto the third and fourth generation of them that hate Me; And showing mercy unto the thousandth generation of them that love Me and keep My commandments.

Thou shalt not take the name of the Lord thy God in vain.

Thou shalt not make unto thee any graven image, or any likeness of any thing that is in heaven above, or that is in the earth beneath, or that is in the water under the earth; Thou shalt now bow down thyself to them, nor serve them; for I the Lord thy God am a jealous God, visiting the iniquity of the fathers upon the children unto the third and fourth generation of them that hate Me; And showing mercy unto thousands of them that love Me, and keep my commandments.

THE THIRD COMMANDMENT

Thou shalt not take the name of the Lord thy God in vain; for the Lord will not hold him guiltless that taketh his name in vain.

Remember thou keep holy the Sabbath Day.

Thou shalt not take the name of the Lord thy God in vain; for the Lord will not hold him guiltless that taketh his name in vain.

THE FOURTH COMMANDMENT

Remember the Sabbath Day to keep it holy. Six days shalt thou labor and do all thy work; but the seventh day is a sabbath unto the Lord thy God, in it thou shalt not do any manner of work, thou, nor thy son, nor thy daughter, nor thy manservant, nor thy maidservant, nor thy cattle, nor thy stranger that is within thy gates; for in six days the Lord made heaven and earth, the sea, and all that in them is, and rested on the seventh day; Wherefore the Lord blessed the sabbath day, and hallowed it.

Honor thy father and mother.

Remember the sabbath day, to keep it holy. Six days shalt thou labor, and do all thy work; But the seventh day is the sabbath of the Lord thy God: in it thou shalt not do any work, thou, nor thy son, nor thy daughter, thy manservant, nor thy maidservant, nor thy cattle, nor thy stranger that is within thy gates: For in six days the Lord made Heaven and Earth, the sea, and all that in them is, and rested the seventh day; wherefore the Lord blessed the sabbath day, and hallowed it.

THE FIFTH COMMANDMENT

Honor thy father and thy mother; that thy days may be long upon the land which the Lord thy God giveth thee.

Thou shalt not kill.

Honor thy father and thy mother; that thy days may be long upon the land which the Lord thy God giveth thee.

THE SIXTH COMMANDMENT

Thou shalt not murder.

Thou shalt not commit adultery.

Thou shalt not kill.

THE SEVENTH COMMANDMENT

Thou shalt not commit adultery.

Thou shalt not steal.

Thou shalt not commit adultery.

THE EIGHTH COMMANDMENT

Thou shalt not steal.

Thou shalt not bear false witness against thy neighbor.

Thou shalt not steal.

THE NINTH COMMANDMENT

Thou shalt not bear false witness against thy neighbor.

Thou shalt not covet thy neighbor's wife.

Thou shalt not bear false witness against thy neighbor.

THE TENTH COMMANDMENT

Thou shalt not covet thy neighbor's house; thou shalt not covet thy neighbor's wife, nor his manservant, nor his maidservant, nor his ox, nor his ass, nor any thing that is thy neighbor's.

Thou shalt not covet thy neighbor's goods.

Thou shalt not covet thy neighbor's house, thou shalt not covet thy neighbor's wife, nor his manservant, nor his maidservant, nor his ox, nor his ass, nor any thing that is thy neighbor's.

THE TEN COMMANDMENTS

As They Appear in "Antiquities of the Jews"

BY

Flavius Josephus

(One of the World's greatest histories, it was
written in 93 A.D. when much of the New
Testament was being created.)

"The First Commandment teaches us that there is but
one God, and that we ought to worship Him only.

"The Second commands us not to make the image of
any living creature to worship it.

"The Third, that we must not swear by God in a false
matter.

"The Fourth, that we must keep the seventh day, by
resting from all sorts of work.

"The Fifth, that we must honour our parents.

"The Sixth, that we must abstain from murder.

"The Seventh, that we must not commit adultery.

"The Eighth, that we must not be guilty of theft.

"The Ninth, that we must not bear false witness.

"The Tenth, that we must not admit of the desire of
any thing that is another's."

BIBLICAL CHAPTER AND VERSE ARRANGEMENTS

THE BIBLICAL quotations in this book are from the three accepted Bibles. The chaptering and the versing of the original Hebrew Version were placed where the translator, in his opinion, judged they belonged. The reader will do well to compare the Hebrew Bible, the King James Version, and the Douay Version.

LEVITICUS 5 (HEBREW)	LEVITICUS 6 (CATHOLIC)	LEVITICUS 6 (PROTESTANT)
20. And the Lord spoke unto Moses, saying:	1. The Lord spoke to Moses, saying:	1. And the Lord spake unto Moses, saying:
21. If any one sin, and commit a trespass against the Lord, and deal falsely with his neighbor in a matter of deposit, or of pledge, or of robbery, or have oppressed his neighbor;	2. Whosoever shall sin and despising the Lord, shall deny to his neighbor the thing delivered to his keeping, which was committed to his trust; or shall by force extort any thing, or commit oppression;	2. If a soul sin, and commit a trespass against the Lord, and lie unto his neighbour in that which was delivered to him to keep, or in fellowship, or in a thing taken away by violence, or hath deceived his neighbour;
22. Or have found that which was lost, and deal falsely therein, and swear to a lie; in any of all these that a man doeth, sinning therein;	3. Or shall find a thing lost, and denying it shall also swear falsely, or shall do any other of the many things, wherein men are wont to sin;	3. Or have found that which was lost, and lieth concerning it, and sweareth falsely; in any of all these that a man doeth sinning therein:

24

LEVITICUS 5
(Hebrew)

LEVITICUS 6
(Catholic)

LEVITICUS 6
(Protestant)

23. Then it shall be, if he hath sinned, and is guilty, that he shall r e s t o r e that which he took by robbery, or the thing w h i c h he hath gotten by oppression, or the deposit w h i c h was deposited with him, or the lost thing which he found,

24. Or anything about w h i c h he hath sworn falsely, he shall even restore it in full, and shall add the fifth part m o r e thereunto; unto him to whom it appertaineth shall he give it, in the day of his being guilty.

4. Being convicted of the offence, he shall restore

5. All that he would h a v e g o t t e n b y fraud, in the principal, and the fifth part besides to the owner, whom he wronged.

4. Then it shall be, because he hath sinned, and is guilty, that he shall restore that which he took violently away, or the thing which he hath deceitfully gotten, or that which w a s delivered t o him to keep, or the lost thing which he found

5. Or all that about w h i c h he h a t h s w o r n falsely; he shall even restore it in the principal, and shall add the fifth p a r t m o r e thereto, *and* give it unto him to whom it appertaineth, in the day of his trespass offering.

ABRIDGMENT OF BIBLICAL LAW

25. We have been careful, that they that will read may have delight, and that they that are desirous to commit to memory might have ease, and that all into whose hands it comes might profit.

26. Therefore to us, that have taken upon us this painful labor of abridging, it was not easy, but a matter of sweat and watching;

27. Even as it is no ease unto him that prepareth a banquet, and seeketh the benefit of others; yet for the pleasuring of many will undertake gladly this great pains;

28. Leaving to the author the exact handling of every particular, and labouring to follow the rules of abridgment.

29. For as the master builder of a new house must care for the whole building; be he that undertaketh to set it out, and paint it, must seek out fit things for the adorning thereof: even so I think it is with us.

30. To stand upon every point, and go over things at large, and to be curious in particulars, belongeth to the first author of the story:

31. But to use brevity, and avoid much laboring of the work, is to be granted to him that will make an abridgment.

32. Here then will we begin the story: only adding thus much to that which hath been said, that it is a foolish thing to make a long prologue, and to be short in the story itself.

ADOPTION

ADOPTION, in the legal sense, is the taking of a stranger into one's family, as a son or daughter. By such action, the adopted person became one's heir. Legal adoption is not recognized by the Common Law of England, and exists in our country by statute.

The various States have adoption laws which generally provide that the person or persons adopting a child or children shall thereafter stand in the place of parent to such as are adopted, and be liable to all the duties and entitled to all the rights of parents. The adopted child becomes an heir-at-law of such persons, the same as if he or she were in fact the natural child of such person.

The right of adoption was known to the ancients of Greece and Rome and was practiced among many nations and peoples from the remotest antiquity.

In Biblical days Mordecai, "when her (Esther) father and mother were dead took her for his own daughter."

It is apparent that in Biblical times there was no formal or so-called legal procedure to be followed in adoption proceedings. It was the intent and act of the person adopting as well as the assent of the person adopted which brought the relationship into existence.

Bible history tells us that where no children were born to a husband and his wife, the wife would direct the husband to cohabit with another woman so that the children of such union would become and be the children of the husband and wife.

And Jacob said unto Joseph . . . thy two sons Ephraim and Manassah, which were born unto thee . . . are mine; as Reuben and Simeon, they shall be mine.   *Genesis 48:3, 5*

Now Sarai Abrams wife bore him no chidren . . . and Sarai . . . took Hagar her maid . . . and gave her to her husband Abram to be his wife . . . it may be that I may obtain children by her. And he went in unto Hagar and she conceived. . . .
                        Genesis 16:1, 2, 3, 4

And when Rachel saw that she bore Jacob no children . . . Rachel said unto Jacob give me children or I die . . . and he said, am I . . . who hath withheld from thee the fruit of the womb? And she said behold my maid Bilhah, go in unto her; and she shall bear upon my knees, that I may also have children by her. And Bilhah conceived, and bore Jacob a son. And Rachel said God hath given me a son.   *Genesis 30:1, 2, 3, 6*

And the daughter of Pharoah came down to wash herself at the river . . . she saw the ark . . . among the flags . . . and she opened it, she saw a child . . . and the child grew . . . and he became her son. And she called his name Moses. . . .
                        Exodus 2:5, 6, 10

And he brought up Hadassah, that is, Esther . . . for she had neither father nor mother . . . (for) Mordecai . . . had taken her for his daughter. . . .   *Esther 2: 7, 15*

AGRICULTURE

OUR STATES and the National Government have created codes of law for the guidance of the farming industry.

When our country was young, its leaders recognized the necessity of education in agriculture. It was evident that more had to be known by the farmer than merely tilling the soil and planting the seed.

In America during the early years of our Government, societies for promoting agriculture were organized in many of the states. These played an important role in the establishment of agricultural colleges. One of the first to be organized was the Philadelphia Society for Promoting Agriculture in 1785. Among its members were George Washington, Noah Webster, and Benjamin Franklin.

It is an accepted practice today to give land a rest from the growing of crops. To many this is a new theory in scientific agricultural development. The Bible anticipated the need for resting the land, and provided in Exodus 23 that all land, producing crops of any kind, be not farmed during every seventh year, thus giving nature an opportunity to replenish the mineral content of the soil. Some writers have thought that this Sabbath year had religious overtones.

Biblical directives and laws dealing with agriculture are even today of basic value. Since food production was of importance to the nomadic Hebrew tribes, it is not surprising that the Bible gives advice and guidance.

THE BIBLICAL LAW

He that tilleth his land shall have plenty of bread. . . .
Proverbs 28:19

Hate not husbandry. . . . *Ecclesiasticus 7:15*

God sent him (Adam) forth from the Garden of Eden, to till
the ground from whence he was taken. *Genesis 3:23*

He that observeth the wind shall not sow; and he that regardeth the clouds shall not reap. *Ecclesiastes 11:4*

The sluggard will not plow by reason of the cold; therefore
shall he beg in harvest, and have nothing. *Proverbs 20:4*

Thou shalt not plow with an ox and an ass together.
Deuteronomy 22:10

. . . he which soweth sparingly shall realp also sparingly; and
he which soweth bountifully shall reap also bountifully.
2 Corinthians 9:6

And six years thou shalt sow thy land, and shalt gather in the
fruits thereof; but the seventh year thou shalt let it rest and lie
still; that the poor of thy people may eat; and what they leave
the beasts of the field shall eat. In like manner thou shalt deal
with thy vineyard, and with thy oliveyard. *Exodus 23:10, 11*

Thou shalt not sow thy vineyard with divers seeds: lest the
fruit of thy seed which thou hast sown, and the fruit of thy vineyard, be defiled. *Deuteronomy 22:9*

Six years thou shalt sow thy field, and six years thou shalt
prune thy vineyard, and gather in the fruit thereof; But in the
seventh year shall be a sabbath of rest unto the land . . . thou
shalt neither sow thy field, nor prune thy vineyard.
Leviticus 25:3, 4

And when ye reap the harvest of your land, thou shalt not wholly reap the corners of thy field, neither shall thou gather the gleanings of thy harvest. And thou shalt not glean thy vineyard, neither shall thou gather every grape of thy vineyard; thou shalt leave them for the poor and stranger. . . .   *Leviticus 19:9, 10*

In the morning sow thy seed, and in the evening withhold not thine hand: for thou knowest not whether shall prosper, either this or that, or whether they both shall be alike good.

Ecclesiastes 11:6

. . . thou shalt not sow thy field with mingled seed. . . .

Leviticus 19:19

Look that thou hedge thy possession about with thorns. . . .

Ecclesiasticus 28:24

Be thou diligent to know the state of thy flocks, and look well to thy herds.   *Proverbs 27:23*

ALIENS

AN ALIEN is any person to whom the rights of citizenship have not been granted by the State in which he resides or sojourns. Aliens in a political sense, are not members of the State although they are subject to the jurisdiction and in a sense clothed with its national character. They are held to owe the State in which they reside allegiance and are bound to obey the laws equally with citizens as well as to carry their share of the public burden.

Being subject to certain obligations and duties, aliens are equally entitled to certain rights and privileges, the most important of which is the right to protection in their persons and property.

The term "citizen" is a different status entirely. In its legal sense it signifies a person who is vested with the freedom and privileges of a city, state or nation as distinguished from a foreigner. The term also signifies one who owes allegiance to, and claims protection from, the city, state, or Government.

The Alien Registration Act of 1940 is said to be the most far-reaching legislation affecting aliens ever enacted in the United States. It requires the registration and fingerprinting of all aliens in the country. When this law was passed by Congress it caused a great furore. Newspapers, magazines and books attacked the unfairness of the legislation. However, it is of moment to note that thousands of years ago, King David and King Solomon did the same thing and required all "foreigners" to be numbered, and thereafter King Solomon "set threescore and ten thousand of them to be bearers of burden, and fourscore thousand to be hewers in the mountain, and three thousand and six hundred overseers to set the people to work."

Mosaic law was created to meet then existing conditions. In every country today like conditions exist. The relationship of Israel with the Phillistines, and other peoples and governments was strained from time to time. The special attention given to aliens was a necessary defense measure. Biblical law, however, directs that strangers, i.e., aliens, are to be treated decently.

THE BIBLICAL LAW

Love ye therefore the stranger: for ye were strangers in the land of Egypt. *Deuteronomy 10:19*

The Lord preserveth the strangers. . . . *Psalms 146:9*

But the stranger that dwelleth with you shall be unto you as one born among you, and thou shalt love him as thyself. . . .
Leviticus 19:34

. . . the sons of the stranger shall not drink thy wine, for which thou hast labored: but they that have gathered it shall eat it . . . and they that brought it together shall drink it. . . .
Isaiah 62:8, 9

Receive a stranger into thine house, and he will disturb thee, and turn thee out of thine own. *Ecclesiasticus 11:34*

And David commanded to gather together the strangers that were in the land of Israel; and he set masons to hew wrought stones to build the house of God. *1 Chronicles 22:2*

. . . your land, strangers devour it in your presence, and it is desolate. . . . *Isaiah 1:7*

Strangers have devoured his strength, and he knoweth it not. . . . *Hosea 7:9*

Lest strangers be filled with thy wealth; and thy labors be in the house of a stranger. *Proverbs 5:10*

And the sons of strangers shall build up thy walls. . . .
Isaiah 60:10

And strangers shall stand and feed your flocks, and the sons of the alien shall be your plowman and your vinedressers.
Isaiah 61:5

And he (Solomon) set threescore and ten thousand of them (aliens) to be bearers of burden, and fourscore thousand to be hewers in the mountain, and three thousand and six hundred overseers to set the people to work.   *2 Chronicles 2:18*

And Solomon numbered all the strangers that were . . . in Israel . . . and they were found an hundred and fifty thousand and three thousand and six hundred.   *2 Chronicles 2:17*

When a stranger shall sojourn with thee, and will keep the passover to the Lord, let all his males be circumcized . . . and he shall be as one that is born in the land. . . .   *Exodus 12:48*

The children that are begotten of them (foreigners) shall enter into the congregation of the Lord in their third generation.
Deuteronomy 23:8

One law shall be to him that is homeborn, and unto the stranger that sojourneth among you.   *Exodus 12:49*

ANIMALS

MUCH ATTENTION was paid to animals during Biblical days. It was commanded that "Thou shalt not let thy cattle gender with a diverse kind," presumably to retain the characteristics of the individual type. On the Sabbath Day the domestic animals must be permitted to rest.

The Bible directs that every man must give assistance to an animal in distress, regardless of whether it belongs to him or to a stranger. One of the unexplained Biblical directives is for the methods of punishing animals for injury done to man. Even as today, the owner is liable for any injury done by an animal, if he has knowledge of the animal's viciousness.

Animal worship prevailed in many parts of the world. In India where it is a consequence of the belief in the transmigration of the soul of a god into the body of an animal. In South America instances of it were met with by the early Spanish conquerors. Its most extraordinary developments were in ancient Egypt, where animals in some parts of the country were regarded as sacred throughout the whole land, and in many cases animals enjoyed a local reverence.

The degree of reverence paid to the sacred animals was such that the voluntary killing of one was punishable with death. It is, therefore, understandable why the Bible in so many instances calls for protection and aid to animals.

The Society for Prevention of Cruelty to Animals in the United States was chartered in 1866 and agitation by similar societies has resulted in laws in almost every state providing for the punishment of cruelty to domestic animals.

THE BIBLICAL LAW

A righteous man regardeth the life of his beast. . . .

Proverbs 12:10

Thou shalt not let the cattle gender with a diverse kind. . . .

Leviticus 19:19

Thou shalt not muzzle the ox when he treadeth out the corn.

Deuteronomy 25:4

But on the seventh day . . . thou shalt not do any work, thou nor . . . thy cattle. . . .   *Exodus 20:8,10*

If thou see the ass of him that hateth thee lying under his burden . . . thou shalt surely help with him.   *Exodus 23:5*

If thou meet thine enemy's ox or his ass going astray, thou shalt surely bring it back to him again.   *Exodus 23:4*

Thou shalt not see thy brother's ass or his ox fall down by the way, and hide thyself from them: thou shalt surely help him to lift them up again.   *Deuteronomy 22:4*

If an ox gore a man or a woman that they die; then the ox shall be surely stoned, and his flesh shall not be eaten: but the owner of the ox shall be quit.   *Exodus 21:28*

But if the ox were wont to push with his horn in time past, and it hath been testified to his owner, and he hath not kept him in, but that he hath killed a man or a woman; the ox shall be stoned, and his owner also shall be put to death. If there be laid on him a sum of money, then he shall give for the ransom of his life whatsoever is laid upon him.   *Exodus 21:29, 30*

If the ox shall push a manservant or a maidservant; he shall give unto their master thirty shekels of silver, and the ox shall be stoned.   *Exodus 21:32*

And if one man's ox hurt another's that he die; then they shall sell the live ox, and divide the money of it; and the dead ox also they shall divide.   *Exodus 21:35*

Or if it be known that the ox hath used to push in time past, and his owner hath not kept him in; he shall surely pay ox for ox, and the dead shall be his own.   *Exodus 21:36*

If a man shall cause a field or vineyard to be eaten, and shall put in his beast, and shall feed in another man's field; of the best of his own field, and of the best of his own vineyard, shall he make restitution.   *Exodus 22:5*

And he that killeth a beast shall make it good; beast for beast. And he that killeth a beast, he shall restore it. . . .
Leviticus 24:18, 21

And if a man shall open a pit, or if a man shall dig a pit, and not cover it, and an ox or an ass fall therein; the owner of the pit shall make it good, and give money unto the owner of them, and the dead beast shall be his.   *Exodus 21:33, 34*

Thou shalt not plow with an ox and an ass together.
Deuteronomy 22:10

Thou shalt not muzzle the ox when he treadeth out the corn.
Deuteronomy 25:4

. . . the good shepherd giveth his life for the sheep.
John 10:11

If a man shall steal an ox, or a sheep, and kill it, or sell it; he shall restore five oxen for an ox, and four sheep for a sheep.
Exodus 22:1

If the theft be certainly found in his hand alive, whether it be ox, or ass, or sheep; he shall restore double. *Exodus 22:4*

BAILMENTS

IN THE LAW today, Bailment, generally, is the delivery of personal property by one person to another for a specific purpose with an agreement that the property be returned or accounted for when the purpose for which it was delivered is accomplished, or until the bailor reclaims it.

When a person receives the goods of another, to keep without recompense, and he acts in good faith, keeping them as his own, he is not answerable for their loss or injury. As he derives no benefit from the bailment, he is responsible only for bad faith or gross negligence.

In bailments for storage or for hire, the bailee acquires a right to defend the property as against third parties and strangers, and is answerable for loss or injury occasioned through his failure to exercise ordinary care.

In the case where cloth is delivered to a tailor to be made up into a garment, the owner does not part with his title, and he may come and take his property after the work has been done, but the workman who has made the garment has a lien upon it for his compensation which, of course, must be reasonable.

There is much similarity in the law today and the law of the Bible.

A people who were constantly on the move had need of laws protecting goods left with and entrusted to those who had a permanent or fixed domicile.

Failure to return property which is entrusted to one's keeping was, under Biblical law, punishable by death.

One who ". . . hath not restored the pledge . . . he shall surely die. . . ." *Ezekiel 18:12, 13*

Today's law is not as severe, providing only for the return of the property, and for damages for the detention; each case, of course, being under the laws made and provided in the several states.

THE BIBLICAL LAW

If a man shall deliver unto his neighbor money or stuff to keep, and it be stolen out of the man's house; if the thief be found, then the master of the house shall be brought unto the judges to see whether he have put his hand unto his neighbor's goods.

. . . so when the judges shall condemn, he shall pay double unto his neighbor.   *Exodus 22:7, 8, 9*

If a man deliver unto his neighbor an ass, or an ox, or a sheep, or any beast, to keep; and it die, or be hurt, or driven away, no man seeing it: Then shall an oath of the Lord be between them both, that he hath not put his hand unto his neighbor's goods; and the owner of it shall accept thereof, and he shall not make it good. And if it be stolen from him, he shall make restitution unto the owner thereof. If it be torn to pieces, then let him bring it for witness, and he shall not make good that which is torn.

Exodus 22:10, 11, 12, 13

And if a soul . . . lie unto his neighbor in that which was delivered him to keep . . . he shall restore it in the principal, and shall add the fifth part more thereto. . . . *Leviticus 6:2, 5*

BRIBERY

IN OUR LAWS, the receiving or giving of a reward to influence the actions of a person in judicial office or in any other office or place of decision is prohibited; particularly, the taking or giving a reward or a bribe to hinder, delay or avoid justice. The accepting of a gift is prohibited not only in our law, but also in the Bible because "the gift blindeth the wise."

Bribery generally is the offering, giving, receiving or soliciting of anything of value with intent to influence the recipient's action as a public official, whether executive, legislative or judicial. The crime includes the acts of soliciting a bribe and attempts to bribe.

Bribery is also the receiving or offering of any undue reward by or to any person whose ordinary profession or business relates to the administration of public affairs in order to incline him to act contrary to the rules of honesty and integrity.

Among ancient peoples, and even as late as the time of the Romans the giving of rewards and emoluments to public officers, especially judicial officers, was tolerated and even encouraged. A later age apprehended the danger, and in modern times the heinousness of the offense became so apparent that the crime has been made punishable as a felony.

Bribery tends to corrupt, and as the law abhors the least tendency to corruption it punishes the act which is calculated to debase and which may affect prejudicially the morals of the community. A public official is the servant of the people. It is his duty impartially to represent the people, and he is not permitted to profit through the performance of his public functions.

In Ecclesiasticus there is the direct admonition that "all bribery shall be blotted out," and the Bible directs:

THE BIBLICAL LAW

Gather not my soul with sinners . . . in whose hands is mischief, and their right hand is full of bribes   *Psalms 26:9, 10*

For I know . . . they take a bribe, and they turn aside the poor . . .   *Amos 5:12*

All bribery . . . shall be blotted out; but true dealing shall endure forever.   *Ecclesiasticus 40:12*

A wicked man taketh a gift . . . to pervert the laws of judgment.   *Proverbs 17:23*

The king by judgment establishes the land: but he that receiveth gifts overthroweth it.   *Proverbs 29:4*

And thou shalt take no gift; for the gift blindeth the wise, and perverteth the words of the righteous.   *Exodus 23:8*

Then . . . Judas Iscariot went unto the chief priests, and said unto them, What will ye give me, and I will deliver him unto you? And they covenanted with him for thirty pieces of silver. And from that time he sought opportunity to betray him.
                                                               Matthew 26:14, 15, 16

And his sons . . . turned aside after lucre, and took bribes, and perverted judgment.   *1 Samuel 8:3*

CONTRACTS

IN AMERICAN LAW, a contract is defined as an agreement by which a person undertakes to do or not to do a particular thing, for a valuable consideration.

In a contract there must be a promise and this promise binds the maker for a future happening, intention or desire.

To create a promise, all that is necessary is that a fair interpretation of the words used shall make it appear that a promise was intended.

Many contracts are mentioned in the Scriptures. One wherein Labin employed Jacob. Jacob by contract offered to work for Labin, and thus buy Labin's younger daughter. Labin accepted the offer saying "it is better that I give her to thee than I give her to another man." After Jacob had served Labin seven years and the agreed time of payment arrived, Labin substituted Leah in place of the younger Rachel, contending that custom required the elder daughter to first be given in marriage. Jacob accepted the substitution and made a second contract to serve seven more years for Rachel, but exacted delivery of Rachel in advance. At the end of this period, he made a third contract to serve Labin for a share of his livestock so that he could get started in his own home and enterprises.

Another contract is that between Pharoh's daughter with the natural mother of Moses to nurse him after he was found in the bulrushes.

The Bible contains many rules, regulations and laws for the creation, maintenance and enforcement of contractual obligations. While it may appear strange that a country of shepherds paid so much attention to contractual liabilities and rights, it was necessary because as Biblical history moved on, the children of Israel became city dwellers and merchants, and acted as middlemen between the nations to the north and those to the south.

A contract for timber (1 Kings 5) between Solomon, King of Israel, and Hyram, King of Tyre, would be by its terms as legally binding today as it was in Biblical times.

Primitive society held that one who was undertaken a duty, in legal form, must fully and exactly perform it, at all events. That a man of full age must take care of himself, and if he has made a foolish bargain he must perform for he had himself to blame. If a man acted, he did so at his own risk. It was his duty to keep his eyes open and abide by the consequences of his agreement.

Laws generally are not now so severe and uncompromising. There are, today, many factors entering into the law of contracts which permit non-performance for fraudulent representation, misrepresentation, inequities, failure of consideration, minority of the person entering into the contract, and many other legal excuses for avoiding the agreement.

THE BIBLICAL LAW

If a man vow a vow . . . or swear an oath to bind his soul with a bond; he shall not break his word, he shall do according to all that proceedeth out of his mouth. *Numbers 30:2*

And Hiram sent to Solomon, saying, I have considered the things which thou sentest to me for; and I will do all thy desire concerning timber of cedar, and concerning timber of fir. My servants shall bring them down from Lebanon unto the sea: and I will convey them by sea in floats unto the place that thou shall appoint me, and will cause them to be discharged there, and thou shall receive them and thou shalt accomplish my desire, in giving food for my household. So Hiram gave Solomon . . . trees . . . and Solomon gave Hiram twenty thousand measures of wheat for food. . . . *1 Kings 5:8, 9, 10, 11*

Keep thy word, and deal faithfully. . . . *Ecclesiasticus 40:12*

For if thy deal truly, thy doings shall prosperously succeed to thee. . . . *Tobit 4:6*

. . . ye should do that which is honest. . . . *II Corinthians 13:7*

. . . do uprightly all thy life. . . . *Tobit 4:5*

He that worketh deceit shall not dwell within my house. . . . *Psalms 101:7*

. . . ye shall not . . . deal falsely. . . . *Leviticus 19:11*

Woe to thee that . . . dealest treacherously and they dealt not treacherously with thee. . . . *Isaiah 33:1*

Have we not all one father? Hath not one God created us? Why do we deal treacherously every man against his brother?. . . . *Malachi 2:10*

Be steadfast in thy understanding; and let thy word be the same. *Ecclesiasticus 5:20*

That which is gone out of thy lips, thou shalt keep and perform. *Deuteronomy 23:23*

CRIME AND PUNISHMENT

THROUGHOUT Biblical literature there are Hebrew words for sin, iniquity, and other synonymous expressions, but no words or phrases such as crime and criminal law in their accepted legal sense. There are only two general classifications: civil cases and cases involving capital punishment. Every offense is termed: transgression.

The absence of the term crime indicates that the will of God is the sole source of all the law, and thus all punishable acts constitute sins which are in violation of God's will.

The Law of Moses contains six hundred and thirteen commandments. Of these, two hundred and forty-eight make the performance of certain acts compulsory. The remaining three hundred and sixty-five prohibit the performance of certain acts.

From the earliest days of recorded history, law-makers and rules appeased the wrath of the Deity by wreaking vengeance not only upon the perpetrator of the crime, but also upon his entire family, parents as well as children.

The Mosaic Law does away with this barbaric practice for in Deuteronomy 24:16—"The fathers shall not be put to death for the children, neither shall the children be put to death for the fathers; every man shall be put to death for his own sin."

In Biblical law, capital punishment has two definitive purposes: (1) retributive, which concerns itself chiefly with rooting out evil by punishing the sinner for his wrong-doing; and (2) deterrent, which makes the punishment so severe that it cannot escape the attention of the public, thereby preventing others from committing a similar act.

Mosaic law provides for thirty-six capital offenses in which number is included adultery, sex perversion, incest, homosexuality, blasphemy, idolatry, false prophecy, profaning the Sabbath, witchcraft, pythonism, sins against parents, kidnapping, treason and murder.

When Ezra, the Scribe, obtained permission from Artaxerxes, King of Babylon, to return with some of the exiled Jews (about 450 B.C.) to the site of old Judea, and there form a new state to be governed by the Law of his God, the authority given by the King to him, permitted only four methods of punishment: death, banishment, confiscation of goods, and imprisonment. The Mosaic law with reference to sin (crime) was unforgiving and harsh.

THE BIBLICAL LAW

. . . there is no man that sinneth not. . . .   *1 Kings 8:46*
Because the law worketh wrath: for where no law is, there
is no transgression.   *Romans 4:15*

. . . sin is not imputed when there is no law. *Romans 5:13*

Woe unto the world because of offences! For it must needs
be that offences come; but woe to that man by whom the
offence cometh.   *Matthew 18:7*

How shall I pardon thee for this? Thy children have forsaken me . . . when I had fed them to the full, they them
committed adultery, and assembled themselves by troops in
the harlots' houses. They were as fed horses in the morning:
every one neighed after his neighbor's wife. *Jeremiah 5:7, 8*

(The Lord) hath commanded no man to do wickedly, neither
hath he given any man license to sin.   *Ecclesiasticus 15:20*

Keep thou far from a false matter . . . for I will not justify
the wicked.   *Exodus 23:7*

If one be found slain in the land . . . lying in the field, and
it be known who hath slain him: Then the elders and thy
judges . . . shall measure unto the cities which are found about
him that is slain . . . and all the elders of that city, that are
next unto the slain man . . . shall answer and say, our hands
have not shed this blood, neither have our eyes seen it.
    Deuteronomy 21:1, 2, 6

When, Pilate . . . asked wether the man (Christ) were a Gali-
lean . . . he knew that he belonged unto Herod's jurisdiction. . . .
    Luke 23:6, 7

For it seemeth to me unreasonable to send a prisoner, and not
withal to signify the crimes laid against him.   *Acts 25:27*

For it is a token of his great goodness, when wicked doers are not suffered any long time, but forthwith punished.

2 Maccabees 6:13

Let me be weighed in an even balance, that God may know mine integrity.

Job 31:6

He that answereth a matter before he heareth it, it is folly and shame unto him.

Proverbs 18:13

Doth our law judge any man, before it hear him, and know what he doeth?

John 7:51

I will hear thee (Paul) when thine accusers are also come. . . .

Acts 23:35

. . . It is not the manner of the Romans to deliver any man to die, before that he which is accused have the accusers face to face, and have license to answer for himself concerning the crime laid against him.

Acts 25:16

And whosoever will not do the law . . . let judgment be executed speedily upon him. . . .

Ezra 7:26

Whoso killeth any person, the murderer shall be put to death by the mouth of witnesses: but one witness shall not testify against any person to cause him to die.

Numbers 35:30

And the judges shall make diligent inquisition; and behold if the witness be a false witness : . . Then shall ye do unto him, as he had thought to have done unto his brother. . . .

Deuteronomy 19:18, 19

If therefore be any pestilent fellows, that have fled from their country unto you, deliver them unto Simon the High Priest, that he may punish them according to their own law.

1 Maccabees 15:21

DAMAGES

WHERE ONE wrongfully or negligently does an act which in its consequences is injurious to another, he is liable for the damage caused by such wrongful act. Damages to be recovered by the claimant must result from a wrong inflicted.

Generally the term "damages" is the sum of money which the law awards or imposes as compensation for an injury done or a wrong sustained. The idea of compensation is fundamental in the conception of damages and the term is used synonymously with compensation.

Ordinarily, nominal damages are recoverable where a right is to be vindicated or where some injury has been done. It is inferred by the law that when there is a breach of an agreement, nominal damages should be awarded plaintiff for an infraction or breach of a contract into which he has entered in good faith.

Biblical law provides for payment of damages. Even as today, Mosaic laws provide for payment of wages lost due to injury, and for the cost of doctors and medication.

If one sustains an injury, either in his person, property or rights, through the act or default of another, he is entitled to receive damages in payment. Punitive damages are levied where injuries are maliciously, recklessly or wantonly inflicted. To constitute the right to recover damages, there must be a loss sustained by the claimant; the defendant must be chargeable with the wrong done, and the loss must be the natural and proximate result of the wrong done.

In the Bible, damages are specifically fixed for each wrong, and are not left to the discretion or judgment of the judge, or as today, the judgment of a jury.

The Bible is mandatory in its laws concerning damages.

THE BIBLICAL LAW

If a man shall steal an ox, or a sheep, and kill it, or sell it; he shall restore five oxen for an ox, and four sheep for a sheep.
Exodus 22:1

If a thief be found . . . he should make full restitution; if he have nohting, then he shall be sold for his theft. *Exodus 22:2, 3*

If the theft be found in his hand alive, whether it be ox, or ass, or sheep, he shall restore double. *Exodus 22:4*

And if a man entice a maid that is not betrothed, and lie with her, he shall surely endow her to be his wife. If her father utterly refuse to give her unto him, he shall pay money according to the doury of virgins. *Exodus 22:16, 17*

And if men strive together, and one smite another with a stone, or with his fist, and he die not, but keepeth his bed: If he rise again, and walk abroad upon his staff, then shall he that smote him be quit; only he shall pay for the loss of his time, and shall cause him to be thoroughly healed.
Exodus 21:18, 19

If a soul . . . commit a trespass . . . and lie unto his neighbor in that which was delivered him to keep, or in fellowship, or a thing taken away by violence, or hath deceived his neighbor;
Or have found that which was lost, and lieth concerning it, and sweareth falsely . . . he shall restore that which he took violently away, or the thing which he hath deceitfully gotten, or that which was delivered to him to keep, or the lost thing which he found.

Or all that about which he hath sworn falsely; he shall even restore it in the principal, and shall add the fifth part more thereto, and give it unto him to whom it appertaineth. . . .
Leviticus 6:2, 3, 4, 5

If a man shall deliver unto his neighbor money or stuff to keep, and it be stolen out of the man's house; if the thief be found, let him pay double. If the thief be not found, then the master of the house shall be brought into the judges, to see whether he have put his hand unto his neighbor's goods.

Exodus 22:7, 8

Men do not despise a thief, if he steal to satisfy his soul when he is hungry; but if he be found, he shall restore sevenfold. . . .

Proverbs 6:30, 31

DEBTORS

BRIEFLY, a debtor is a person who owes something to another, or to others. Debt is an obligation to pay or return something.

Debt denotes not only the obligation to pay, but also the right of the creditor to receive as well as enforce payment. Everything is a debt which is an obligation on the person to perform. Debt is synonymous with due; both are derived from the same verb.

Becoming a debtor has, through the history of man, been easy of accomplishment and therefore the law has taken into consideration the wilfulness of those who are holders of obligations of others and has provided that the lender shall not burden the debtor beyond what is reasonable for the use of the money or property involved.

Usury is defined as an unlawful contract upon the loan of money to receive the same again with exorbitant increase, but generally, usury is actually the receiving, securing or taking of a greater sum or value for the loan of money, goods or things in action than is allowed by the existing law. Many states have enacted laws limiting the highest rate of interest to be charged.

In those places where a usury law has been adopted, a limitation is set on the amount of interest to be paid and in the cases where there is a greater amount exacted than the law allows, punitive penalties have been attached to the receiving of exorbitant amounts.

The common law of England which is basically followed in this country, did not have a law against usurious interest on money or things loaned; even though most of the common law is predicated on the Mosaic law, which prohibits usurious interest.

Deuteronomy 15:6 easily solves the problem of debt: "Thou shalt not borrow."

... thou shalt not borrow. ...   *Deuteronomy 15:6*

Be not made a begger by banqueting upon borrowing, when thou hast nothing in thy purse. ...   *Ecclesiasticus 18:33*

He that buildeth his house with other men's money is like one that gathered himself stones for the tomb of his burial.
Ecclesiasticus 21:8

... the borrower is servant to the lender.   *Proverbs 22:7*

... from him that would borrow of thee turn not thou away.
Matthew 5:42

Lose thy money for thy brother and thy friend, and let it not rust under a stone to be lost.   *Ecclesiasticus 29:10*

Lend not unto him that is mightier than thyself; for if thou lendest him, count it but lost.   *Ecclesiasticus 8:12*
Owe no man anything. ...   *Romans 13:8*

Usury

If thou lend money to any of my people that is poor by thee, thou shalt not be to him as an usurer, neither shall thou lay upon him usury.   *Exodus 22:25*

(He that) hath given forth upon usury, and hath taken increase ... shall surely die. ...   *Ezekiel 18:13*

Thou shalt not lend upon usury to thy brother; usury of money, usury of victuals, usury of anything that is lent upon usury:

Unto a stranger thou mayest lend upon usury; but unto thy brother thou shalt not lend upon usury. ...
Deuteronomy 23:19, 20

Repayment

.He that is hasty to give credit is lightminded. . . .
Ecclesiasticus 19:4

Let not thine hand be stretched out to receive, and shut when thou shouldest repay.   *Ecclesiasticus 4:31*

And forgive us our debts, as we forgive our debtors.
Matthew 6:12

. . . for we also forgive everyone that is indebted to us.
Luke 11:4

Greed

. . . thou hast taken usury and increase, and thou hast greedily gained of thy neighbors by extortion. . . .   *Ezekiel 22:12*

. . . he that maketh haste to be rich shall not be innocent.
Proverbs 28:20

For the love of money is the root of all evil. . . .
1 Timothy 6:10

Be not greedy to add money to money. . . .   *Tobit 5:18*

Statute of Limitations

At the end of every seven years thou shalt make a release . . . Every creditor that lendeth ought unto his neighbor shall release it; he shall not exact it of his neighbor, or of his brother. . . .
Deuteronomy 15:1, 2

Banks

Wherefore then gavest not thou my money into the bank, that at my coming I might have required mine own with usury?
Luke 19:23

DEFENSES

THE VARIOUS DEFENSES for the almost limitless number of subjects in the law cannot be discussed in a book of this kind. It is sufficient that under the various headings hereinafter found there will be discussed many general, special, and specific defenses to various sins which we term crimes.

In Genesis, Adam defends himself from the sin of eating of the Tree of Life, by blaming the woman whom God gave to him, and the woman, in turn, blamed the serpent.

It is interesting to observe that in Biblical times too man sought to avoid responsibility for crime or for the commission of an act which was not in accordance with the accepted standards of the community.

Law makers from time immemorial have not only created crimes and punishments, but realized the weakness and frailty of mankind and set standards of defense to excuse, justify or vindicate.

Among defenses permitted by Biblical law is, committing an act through ignorance "but the soul that doeth aught presumptuously shall be cut off from his people."

The defense of mental inadequacy was not known to the Bible, nor is any mental deficiency recognized. There was, however, the right to be confronted by an accuser before it was necessary to defend. Basically, the law today is a repetition and refinement of Mosaic law.

THE BIBLICAL LAW

The woman whom thou gavest to be with me, she gave me
of the tree, and I did eat.   *Genesis 3:12*

And the woman said, the serpent beguiled me, and I did eat.
                                               Genesis 3:13

And if any soul sin through ignorance . . . the priest shall
make an atonement . . . and it shall be forgiven him. But the
soul that doeth ought presumptuously . . shall be cut off from
among his people.   *Numbers 15:27, 28, 30*

And that servant, which knew his Lord's will, and . . . neither
did according to his will, shall be beaten with many stripes. But
he that knew not . . . shall be beaten with few stripes.
                                          Luke 12:47, 48

. . . Our hands have not shed this blood, neither have our eyes
seen it. . . .   *Deuteronomy 21:7*

. . . if ye put me to death, ye shall surely bring innocent blood
upon yourselves. . . .   *Jeremiah 26:15*

. . . hear ye my defence, which I make now unto you.
                                               Acts 22:1

What have I offended against thee, or against thy servants,
or against this people, that ye have put me in prison?
                                          Jeremiah 37:18

Save me from all them that persecute me, and deliver me.
                                               Psalms 7:1

. . . deliver me from the hand of mine enemies, and from them
that persecute me.   *Psalms 31:15*

. . . he remembered not to show mercy, but persecuted the
poor and needy man, that he might even slay the broken in heart.
                                          Psalms 109:16

Persecuted, but not forsaken; cast down, but not destroyed.
2 Corinthians 4:9

Blessed are they which are persecuted for righteousness' sake: for theirs is the kingdom of heaven. *Matthew 5:10*

... my persecutors shall stumble, and they shall not prevail. ...
Jeremiah 20:11

And Samuel said unto all Israel ... Behold here I am: witness against me before the Lord . . . whose ox have I taken? Or whose ass have I taken? Or whom have I defrauded? Whom have I oppressed? Or of whose hand have I received any bribe to blind my eyes therewith? And I will restore it to you.
1 Samuel 12:1, 3

And the scribes and Pharisees brought unto him (Jesus) a woman taken in adultery ... They say to him . . . Moses in the law commanded us, that such be stoned: but what sayest thou? . . . and [Jesus] said unto them, He that is without sin among you, let him first cast a stone at her. *John 8:3, 4, 5, 7*

Former Jeopardy

And the righteous [i.e. he that was once declared to be righteous] slay thou not. *Exodus 23:7*

DIVORCE

UNDER MOSAIC LAW, a husband could divorce his wife by giving her a Bill of Divorcement and sending her out of his house whenever he found some uncleanness in her. The dissolution of the marriage thus brought about was absolutely final so that even the wife was free to marry again.

The teachings of the Christian faith, however, have led to restrictions concerning divorce, but by the general civil law, either party could abrogate the marriage contract, first at the pleasure of the one desiring to do so, and later for reasons granted by the law.

Denying of divorce under certain circumstances and conditions creates hatreds, miseries and crimes which result and flow from indissoluable marital connections, but no law has ever gone so far as to subject marriage to dissolution by the mutual will of the parties.

Sir William Blackstone in his Commentaries on the Common Law said that divorces were within the cognizance of the Ecclesiastical courts only, and were of two kinds—the one total and the other partial. The total divorce was always for some one of the cannonical causes such as consanguinity or affinity. The partial divorce was allowed when for some cause it became improper or impossible for the parties to live together.

The Common Law of England and the Ecclesiastical law of that country were never adopted in this country. Here it is the province of the legislature of the several states to regulate the subject of divorce as applied to their citizens and persons domiciled within their jurisdiction. The power of the Legislature over the subject of marriage and over the matter of its dissolution is unlimited and supreme, subject of course, to the constitutional restriction that each community shall not pass any local or special law granting divorces.

Every person has the right to seek and obtain a divorce, but must do so under the statutes of the several states. Divorce is not a right, but is solely granted by general laws enacted for that purpose.

Divorce is the ending of the marriage relation other than by death. An annulment differs from a divorce; it may be had for causes existing before or at the time of marriage and which go to the very essence of the marital relation, such as the wife committed fornication and was pregnant by another, or that she concealed her sterility, or that one or both of the parties was not legally capable of marrying, or that the husband was impotent.

Biblical law is without equivocation in matters of divorce. It can be accepted as fact that the tribal laws and regulations of the Hebrews were directed toward the permanency of the family and its necessity in the life of the nation.

Since Biblical days, cause for divorce has been enlarged. Today the most often used is "extreme cruelty"; a term which may mean almost anything.

Generally it is the wrongful infliction of grievous bodily injury, or grievous mental suffering by one spouse on the other. Each case must be determined on its own facts and circumstances. Since the disposition, habit and custom varies from person to person, it is not possible for the legislature or the courts to precisely define a universal rule. A decision by the court must depend on the sound judgment and "common sense" of the trial court.

What is cruelty, is difficult to state comprehensively; some courts are far more lenient than others, but the reason of the difference lies in the varying views the courts take of the marital relation and of its place in the social polity. Cruelty is such conduct in one of the married parties as, to the reasonable apprehension of the other, or in fact, renders cohabitation physically unsafe, to a degree justifying a withdrawal therefrom. The actual use or the apprehension of violence is considered necessary; or perhaps it would more faithfully represent the position of some of our conservative courts to say, that although violence be pronounced essential, yet acts are now placed under the head of violence which were not so regarded by the earlier judges. The reason for granting a divorce for this cause at all is in the fact that courts of law will not compel a person to live with one from whom injury is to be feared. It is not so much to punish an offense already committed as to relieve the complaining party from apprehended danger.

A classical discussion of this subject is found in an 1836 decision of a New Hampshire court:

"The parties in this case were married in March, 1816. They have no children. The husband is proved to be a man in easy circumstances, and of a hasty and irritable temper. The wife is shown to be a very active and efficient manager of her household affairs, and of a high, bold, masculine spirit; somewhat impatient of control; in a high degree jealous of the liberty that belongs to her as a wife, and not always ready to submit, even to the legitimate authority of her husband. For aught that appears in this case, they lived in peace and harmony until some time since the year 1830, when the wife, having become a professor of religion, united herself to a church whose doctrines and opinions the husband did not approve.

66

This diversity of sentiments in religious matters seems to have been the original fountain whence has flowed all the bitterness which has since existed between them, and which has driven them into quarrels, squabbles and encounters, that certainly do no credit to either party. The result of these broils was, that the wife left the house of the husband, and has since resided separate and apart from him; and she now seeks to have the bonds of matrimony dissolved, on the ground that in the contest which ended in their separation, he exercised a tyranny over her which amounted to extreme cruelty.

In a contest about religion between two persons standing in the relation, and having the dispositions and tempers of these parties, it is hardly to be conceived that the blame could have been all on one side. Mere profession of religion weighs nothing in such a case If the spirit of the gospel abide with one of the parties, not in word only but in its power, there can be no contest; whatever wrong or injury there may be on the one side—all will be patience and suffering on the other. Where strife is, there is every evil work. But that wisdom which is from above is first pure, then peaceable, gentle, and easy to be entreated, full of mercy and good fruits. This is the language of inspiration.

The evidence in this case shows much strife between these parties; and an attentive examination of that evidence will enable us to see who has been to blame.

One of the complaints of the wife in this case is that the husband has often addressed her in harsh, abusive, and profane language. This charge is sustained by the evidence, and his conduct in this respect can be viewed in no other light than as unmanly, indecorous, and in the highest degree reprehensible. And in the case of a woman of a meek and quiet spirit, incapable of rendering evil for evil, or railing for railing, but patient in all her tribulations, such language on the part of a husband, often repeated, wantonly and unprovoked, would go a great way, and be a circumstance of much weight, in making out a case of extreme cruelty.

But here much of the evidence on both sides, and even the tone and temper of the affidavit which she has drawn up herself and filed in the case, indicate in the wife anything rather than a meek and quiet spirit. And one of her own witnesses says that her conduct was often provoking and vexatious. She herself admits, in her affidavit, that she sometimes used passionate language, but says she used it only when he gave her occasion. It is very likely that she may think she had always an occasion for the passionate language she used; and it is equally likely that he may think he had an occasion for the harsh and abusive language he used towards here. It is not proved that he used such language wantonly and unprovoked on any occasion. And if a wife chooses so to act and to talk as to raise a storm in the temper of an irritable husband, it is doing her no injustice to say to her, when it has come attended only with harsh and abusive language, that she has had in its peltings her just and merited reward. However reprehensible his conduct may have been in this respect, she is not to be heard, when she would complain of it. She ought not to be heard to complain of abuse which she has wantonly provoked.

Her next complaint grows out of a contest between them with respect to some wood, in August, 1833. Her story is that she sent a little girl out to procure some wood—that the husband met the girl at the door and told her "she should not"—that she then went herself for the wood, and as she went out, he went into the house. When she returned she found the door fastened—upon which she threw her wood into the house through the window, and took a crowbar and knocked at the door; that he came out in a great passion, and using very profane language, which she repeats, but which we shall not, took the crowbar from her by force; that she screamed murder, and he stopped her mouth. But at length she escaped, and soon after deserted the house.

Now in this account it is virtually admitted that she went out in open rebellion against the known will of her husband. And the throwing of the wood into the house by the window, the use she made of the crowbar, and her screams of murder when he took the bar from her, indicate a spirit and temper quite too belligerent, when indulged against a husband, to be becoming in a lady. But her witness adds other material circumstances, which she has omitted, and says that the husband told the girl not to take the wood that was on the other side of the road, but to take it from the mill-house, because he wanted to clear that—that upon this the wife came out and said that she sent the girl, and intended to have the wood. He further says, that she struck the door with the crowbar and made several dents in it, which are still visible; and that after the husband took the bar from her she threatened to go to a magistrate and compel him to give sureties of the peace, and that he told her that she had better go into the house.

Such is the transaction, as it stands disclosed in the evidence. There seems to have been nothing unreasonable or improper in the direction which the husband gave to the little girl. And the temper in which the wife went forth from the house, and her declared intention of having her own will and her own way, in defiance of him, which was immediately carried into overt acts of rebellion against his authority, show her to have been entirely in the wrong on that occasion. She was to blame in the beginning: and she carried out the quarrel in a manner which all candid and impartial minds must pronounce to have been equally inconsistent with her connubial duties and her religious professions. In the skirmish which ended in his taking the crowbar from her, she seems to have been rather roughly handled. But considering the irritable temper of the husband, it seems to us that she escaped with quite as little injury as she could have had any right to expect, in such an attempt to take his castle by storm.

Her next complaint is founded upon a quarrel between her and her husband which took place upon the Sabbath. The account which she gives of the matter in her affidavit is, that she asked him to let her have the horse and chaise to go to church. This he refused, because he did not like the minister. She then ordered the boy to put the horse to the chaise, and went out herself to the chaise-house to assist the boy. Finding the chaise-house locked, she requested him to let her have the key, which he refused. She thereupon took hold of the door, "and made as though she would open it." Upon this, the husband came out and struck her upon the head, and made her head ache for several days. Such is her account of the affair. But her witness states other material circumstances, which she omits. He says that she went out to the chaise-house and attempted to force the lock with a wedge; that the husband came out, and took the wedge from her, and ordered her to go into the house. She, however, still persisted in her attempt to obtain the chaise, until he struck her.

Now, in this instance, the quarrel had its origin in the misconduct of the husband. No good reason is shown why the use of the horse and chaise should not have been freely accorded to her. And his refusal of her reasonable request, not only has the appearance of great unkindness, but of a tyrannical attempt to embarrass her in the enjoyment of that religious liberty which belongs to every wife.

But it was the Sabbath—and, under the circumstances, what course of conduct did duty prescribe to a Christian wife and to a member of the church? The very essence of the religion she professes is, that charity suffereth long and is kind, which vaunteth not itself, doth not behave unseemly, is not easily provoked, and not only believeth and hopeth, but beareth and endureth all things. What course of conduct, then, did duty prescribe to one who professed to have adopted that religion as the guide of her life? If when ye do well and suffer for it, yet take it patiently, this is acceptable with God, says the Bible. What course of conduct did duty then prescribe to one who professes to believe the Bible to be the word of God? In my judgment, there cannot be any diversity of opinion on these questions. It was due to the day, it was due to the religion she professes, it was due to the relation in which she stood to her oppressor, that, if she could not obtain his consent by kindness and condescension, she should have submitted in silence to the wrong he was doing her. But instead of this, regardless of the day and of the modesty and of all the sober virtues that belong to the character of a pious matron, at the head of a respectable family, and setting her husband completely at defiance, she at once undertook to accomplish her purpose by force and violence; and in this course she persisted, until, provoked by her perverse obstinacy, the husband was led so far to forget himself as to strike her.

Whatever the old books may say upon the subject, there never was, in my opinion, in the relation between husband and wife, when rightly understood, anything

71

that gave to a husband the right to reduce a refractory wife to obedience by blows. And at this day the moral sense of the community revolts at the idea that a husband may inflict personal chastisement upon his wife, even for the most outrageous conduct. The blow given by the husband in this case deserved the severest censure. All must condemn it. But I am much mistaken if the stubborn obstinacy with which the wife set him at defiance, and the violence she used in her rebellion against his authority, will not, under all the circumstances, be quite as revolting to the moral sense of an enlightened and a religious community as the unmanly conduct of the husband.

She further complains of personal violence, inflicted by the husband in the quarrel about making matches. The account she gives of the transaction in her affidavit is, that while she was making the matches, according to his directions, and obeying him in all things, he, without any provocation, became violently enraged, and having beaten her cruelly with a horsewhip, imprisoned her in the cellar. The story is confirmed in some particulars by one witness who says he heard a dispute between the parties, and two blows of a whip, and saw her come up from the cellar, and by another witness who says he saw the husband strike her two or three times with a whip, but not very heavily. He also saw him carry her into the cellar. This witness further says that the parties talked very angrily. Still another witness says she heard blows of a whip and afterwards saw marks of violence upon the person of plaintiff.

She has another complaint of personal chastisement, inflicted by the husband, in the dispute about certain papers belonging to the society for educating pious young men, of which society she was treasurer. Her account of this affair is, that the husband took the papers from her drawer and put them into his desk; that she demanded them, and he refused to restore them; that a few days afterwards she had an opportunity to obtain possession of them, in his absence, and took them away. When he came home and was informed of this, he flew into a violent passion, and using very profane and abusive language, finally horsewhipped her. Her account is, in some reports, confirmed by the testimony of a witness.

Such is the case presented by the evidence laid before us on the part of the wife. And I shall, in the first place, consider whether, upon the case thus presented, she is entitled to the decree she asks. It then becomes necessary to consider the true nature of the relation between husband and wife, and what is to be deemed extreme cruelty, within the meaning and intent of the statute.

In scripture the wife is represented as standing, in some respects, in the same relation to the husband as the husband stands to the Redeemer, and the Redeemer to God. The words are: The head of every man is Christ, and the head of the woman is the man, and the head of Christ is God. And in our law the wife is considered as being, in some respects, subordinate to the husband, who is the head of the house. The husband and wife are, in the contemplation of the law, one. Her legal existence and authority are suspended during the continuance of the matrimonial union. He is bound to support and maintain her in a manner suitable to her situation and his condition. He is made answerable for her debts contracted before the marriage. And during the continuance of the union he alone is responsible for crimes committed by her in his presence—the law not considering her, in such a case, as acting by her own will, but by his compulsion. He is answerable for all torts and frauds committed by her; and if committed in his company he alone is answer-

73

able. And she is wisely made subject in many thing to his authority, as he is subject to the laws under which he lives. But a wife is neither the slave nor the servant of a husband. He is the head of the house, to whom as such she is subordinate. But she is at the same time his companion, the partner and sharer of his fortune, in many respects his equal; who in her appropriate sphere is entitled to share largely in his authority.

He is bound, not only to honor and support her, but to accord to her freely and liberally all her rights, and to guarantee to her the full and free enjoyment of all her just privileges and prerogatives as the mistress of the family.

He is bound to leave her free to enjoy her own religious opinions, and worship God according to the dictates of her own reason and conscience; and not to molest or restrain her in this respect, provided she does not in her zeal disturb the public peace, nor rebel against his lawful authority. Such is the equality and dignity which our laws confer upon the female character; and such the relation in which husband and wife stand to one another.

What then is extreme cruelty? It is not mere austerity of temper, petulance of manners, rudeness of language, a want of civil attention, or even occasional sallies of temper, if there be no threat of bodily harm. It is not the denial of little indulgencies or particular accommodations. Such denial may in many cases be extremely unkind and unhandsome, and disgraceful to the character of a husband, and yet not amount to the cruelty intended by the statute. To constitute extreme cruelty in a husband, his misconduct must be such as to show that the inward knot of marriage, which is peace and love, is untied, and that he exercises over his wife, not the mild and salutary authority of a husband, but a harsh and cruel tyranny. In the judgment of the law, any willful misconduct of the husband, which endangers the life or the health of the wife; which exposes her to bodily hazard and intolerable hardship, and renders cohabitation unsafe, is extreme cruelty.

In order to amount to such cruelty it is not necessary that there should be many acts. Whenever force and violence, preceded by deliberate insult and abuse, have been once wantonly and without provocation used, the wife can hardly be considered as safe. But it is a well-settled rule, that a wife is not entitled to be divorced on the ground of ill treatment received from her husband, if that ill treatment has been drawn upon her by her own misconduct. The cruelty which lays a just and legal foundation for a divorce, must be unmerited and unprovoked. When she is ill treated on account of her own misconduct, her remedy is in a reform of her manners, unless the return from the husband is wholly unjustified by the provocation, and quite out of proportion to the offense.

Such are the rules of law that are to govern this decision; and there is very little difficulty in the application of them to the facts in this case. With respect to the quarrels and contests between the parties about the wood, and about the horse and chaise, there is no doubt. Whatever may have been the ill treatment which the wife received on those occasions it is very manifest she drew it down upon herself by her obstinacy and ill conduct. Nor does the return made by the husband appear to have been much out of proportion to the offense.

With regard to the quarrel about the matches, it is very clear that such was the conduct of the husband on that occasion, that if it is to be considered as altogether wanton and unprovoked, it entitles the libelant to the decree she asks. To beat a wife with a whip, and then put her in-

75

to the cellar without any provocation, is both unjust and tyrannical; and, even in a case of great provocation, it could hardly be considered as manly conduct. It is not denied that he struck her with a whip, or that he put her into the cellar; and she states in her affidavit that she gave him no provocation whatever. This, however, is denied by him in his affidavit. The parties were alone when the quarrel began, and no other person knows in what it originated. It is proved that both very soon became very angry. It is not at all probable that all the fault was on one side. Nor is it likely that he would have proceeded to blows if there was no provocation, but all was submission on her part. The proofs which are in the case of her conduct and spirit on other occasions, render it quite improbable that she was at this time beaten and abused for her meekness and condescension. Besides, we have had an opportunity to compare her accounts of other transactions between herself and her husband, with the accounts which her witnesses give of the same transactions; and this comparison shows very clearly, that however fair her general character for truth and veracity may be, very little reliance can be placed upon her statements, when they relate to her disputes with her husband.

Perhaps it would be too much to expect that she should, under the circumstances, give a full and fair account of those transactions. It is certain, if her witnesses are to be believed, her accounts are neither full nor fair; and we cannot presume that her account of the occurrence we are now considering, is perfectly correct. We entirely condemn the use of the whip by the husband, as unlawful and unmanly. But no very serious injury was done to her person; and her own affidavit, unsupported as it is by any other testimony, has failed to satisfy us that the conduct of the husband was wanton, unprovoked, and unmerited, which is essential, to make it a legal ground of a divorce.

Indeed, taking all the testimony together, it seems to us to be rather more probable, on the whole, that she may have designedly used means to provoke him to acts of violence, in order that she might have a pretense for leaving him, than that, wantonly and unprovoked, he inflicted personal chastisement upon her. The same remarks, to a very great extent, are applicable in all their force to the quarrel between the parties about the papers belonging to the society for educating pious young men. The parties were alone during the whole contest, and they alone know the spirit and temper in which it proceeded. There are, however, two circumstances to be considered in this instance, which did not exist in the contest about the matches. The wife was the treasurer of the society, and to take the papers from her without her consent and lock them up in his desk, certainly had the appearance, not only of unkindness, but of an unmanly meddling in a concern which was exclusively under the management of the ladies who belonged to the society, and must have been calculated to vex and irritate the wife. On the other hand, her taking advantage of his absence to open the desk and take away the papers, has in it too much of a disposition to have her own will, and her own way, by foul means if not by fair, to be commended in a wife, and was calculated to exasperate her husband.

Now, considering the temper and disposition this lady is proved to have exhibited on other occasions, what is the probability as to her course of conduct when the husband came to reproach her for taking away the papers from his desk in his absence? Did she endeavor to avert the gathering storm by meek and submissive behavior, or did she retort upon him as unmanly interference in the concerns of a female society, with which he had nothing to do? It seems to us much more probable that he was driven to violence by her provoking taunts—taunts which may have been the more provoking, because he felt in them the sting of truth and justice—than that he should have resorted to blows without any new provocation on her part at that time. And this presumption is much strengthened by the consideration that the husband although quick and hasty in his temper, does not seem to be naturally vindictive; while the wife is shown to have been at other times quite as busy and active in a quarrel with her husband, as in the management of her ordinary household affairs. And we are of opinion, on the whole, that however obnoxious to censure the conduct of the husband may have been on any, or on all the occasions to which we have averted, the wife has no right to complain; because it is in the highest degree probable that in every instance she drew upon herself the chastisement she received, by her own improper conduct. And it does not appear that on any occasion the injury she received was much out of proportion to her offense.

Her remedy is to be sought, then, not in this court, but in a reformation of her own manners. Let her return to the path of duty; and if to a discreet and prudent exercise of her just rights and privileges as a wife, she will join that meekness, patience, and kindness which the religion she professes inculcates, and temper all her conduct towards her husband with that sweetness and goodness which belong to the true character of a wife, we think she will have no reasonable ground to apprehend any further injury to her person. Let her submit to the authority of her husband, and remember that the dignity of a wife cannot be violated by such submission. Let her return to the path of duty; and by displaying in all her conduct the mild and gentle spirit of the gospel, make that path a path of peace and safety.

And let the husband recollect that the first duty of the head of a family is to be master of himself, and to have his temper and feelings in due subjection to his reason and understanding, so that no provocation shall drive him, on any occasion, to unjust and unmanly acts of violence, or even to the use of profane and abusive language. And remembering his own infirmities let him generously go forward, and not only invite but encourage his wife to return to her duty, by satisfactory assurances, not only that her person shall be safe, but that her feeling shall not be insulted again by profane or abusive language, and that her religious rights shall not be in any way abridged. And let all those who attempt to advise them, consider who it is that has said, "Blessed are the peacemakers, for they shall be called the children of God.

Between these parties there is much to be forgotten and forgiven on both sides. But if they shall be disposed to retrace their steps; and if those who are around them shall aid and encourage them in all their attempts at reconcilation, it is to be hoped that they will encounter no serious obstacle in finding their way back to domestic peace and happiness."

. . . let none deal treacherously against the wife of his youth.
Malachi 2:15

When a man hath taken a wife, and married her, and it come to pass that she find no favor in his eyes, because he hath found some uncleanness in her; then let him write her a bill of divorcement, and give it in her hand, and send her out of his house.
Deuteronomy 24:1

And when she is departed . . . she may go and be another man's wife. And if the latter husband write her a bill of divorcement . . . or if the latter husband die . . . her former husband . . . may not take her again to be his wife.
Deuteronomy 24:1, 2, 3, 4

If she go not as thou wouldest have her, cut her off from thy flesh, and give her a bill of divorce, and let her go.
Ecclesiasticus 25:26

But I say unto you, that whosoever shall put away his wife, saving for the cause of fornication, causeth her to commit adultery: and whosover shall marry her that is divorced commiteth adultery.
Matthew 5:32

. . . What therefore God hath joined together, let no man put asunder.
Matthew 19:6

An evil wife is a yoke shaken to and fro: he that hath hold of her is as though he held a scorpion *Ecclesiasticus 26:7*

Let not the wife depart from her husband. *1 Corinthian 7:10*
For the woman which hath an husband is bound by the law to her husband as long as he liveth. . . . *Romans 7:2*

If any brother hath a wife that believeth not, and she be pleased to dwell with him, let him not put her away. And the woman which hath an husband that believeth not, and if he be pleased to dwell with her, let her not leave him.
1 Corinthians 7:13, 14

Whosoever putteth away his wife, and marrieth another, committeth adultery: and whosoever marrieth her that is put away from her husband committeth adultery. *Luke 16:18*

. . . where is the bill of your mother's divorcement, whom I have put away? *Isaiah 50:1*

I had rather dwell with a lion and a dragon, than to keep house with a wicked woman. *Ecclesiasticus 25:16*

DRINKING

THE ORIGIN of the word "alcohol" is somewhat obscure. However, the drinking problem has been of importance in every organized society. From time to time prohibition movements against the use of intoxicating liquors have been enacted and repealed. In some countries organizations commonly known as the Prohobition Party, and in some as the Anti-Saloon League, and like organizations, have been urging national prohibition.

There has always been concern about drinking of alcoholic beverages to excess. The Bible is replete with references to the drinking of wine, and reminds constantly that wine is as good as life to a man if it be drunk moderately. In Proverbs it is written "give strong drink unto him that is ready to perish and wine unto those that be of heavy hearts."

It is not understandable how laws forcing men to refrain from drinking can be enforced any more than laws which direct man to drink. Moderation is a matter of personal choice, and whether it is the law of the Bible, or the law today, no regulation can accomplish that which the human will does not desire.

Moderation is what the Bible seeks in its mandates, and its cautionary advice is best said in Proverbs 23: "look not thou upon the wine when it is red . . . it biteth like a serpent and stingeth like an adder."

THE BIBLICAL LAW

Wine is as good as life to a man, if it be drunk moderately. . . .
Ecclesiasticus 31:27

Give strong drink unto him that is ready to perish, and wine unto those that be of heavy hearts. Let him drink, and forget poverty, and remember his misery no more. *Proverbs 31:6, 7*

Drink no longer water, but use a little wine for thy stomach's sake and thine often infirmities.   *1 Timothy 5:23*

. . . it is hurtful to drink wine or water alone; wine mingled with water is pleasant, and delighteth the taste. . . .
2 Maccabees 15:39

It is good neither . . . to drink wine . . . whereby thy brother tumbleth, or is offended, or is made weak.   *Romans 14:21*

. . . it is not for kings to drink wine; nor for princes strong drink: lest they drink and forget the law, and pervert the judgement of any of the afflicted.   *Proverbs 31:4, 5*

Shew not thy valiantness in wine; for wine has destroyed many.
Ecclesiasticus 31:25

And he drank of the wine, and was drunken; and he was uncovered (indecent exposure) within his tent.   *Genesis 9:21*

For a bishop must be blameless . . . a lover of . . . good men, sober . . . temperate.   *Titus 1:7, 8*

Wherefore gird up the loins of your mind, be sober.
1 Peter 1:13

Meekness, temperance: against such there is no law.
Galatians 5:23

. . . drink not wine to make thee drunken: neither let drunkenness go with thee in thy journey.   *Tobit 4:15*

Drunkenness increaseth the rage of a fool till he offend: it diminisheth strength, and maketh wounds.

Ecclesiasticus 31:30

Woe unto them that rise up early in the morning that they may follow strong drink; that continue till night, till wine inflame them. *Isaiah 5:11*

Do not drink wine nor strong drink . . . when ye go into the tabernacle of the congregation. . . . *Leviticus 10:9*

Look not thou upon the wine when it is red . . . it biteth like a serpent, and stingeth like an adder. *Proverbs 23:31, 32*

A laboring man that is given to drunkeness shall not be rich. . . . *Ecclesiasticus 19:1*

Woe unto him that giveth his neighbor drink . . . and makest him drunken also. . . . *Habakkuk 2:15*

. . . the priest and the prophet have erred through strong drink. . . . *Isaiah 28:7*

And every man that striveth for the mastery is temperate in all things. *1 Corinthians 9:25*

ECONOMICS

THE BIBLE contains law concerning possessions and their acquisition. In one of the ten commandments . . . "thou shalt not covet thy neighbor's house"—unlawful acquisition is prohibited.

Isaiah says "Woe unto them that join house to house, that lay field to field until there be no place, that they may be placed alone in the midst of the earth." It must be assumed that this is the first law against the appropriation of large grants of land to the exclusion of the general public.

England, France and Canada divided most of the land among the powerful families who financed the expeditions to the so-called "new world." Times have changed since then, and now the average man is able to acquire land in his own right.

Biblical law provides for the division of land among the twelve tribes of Israel, but whether it was apportioned to each family is not clear.

Exodus 23:10, 11 provides for a Sabbath year. Its object was not economic, to increase the fertility of the soil, but religious, to acknowledge God's ownership of the land by renouncing its use every seventh year.

In accordance with the directive in Exodus 23:19—"The first of the first fruits of thy land thou shalt bring unto the house of the Lord thy God," which may indicate that all ownership was subject to the will of God, and that the management of the affairs of government as well as the needs of the individual were religious rather than legal or political.

There were only two classes in the Holy Land; the rich, and the poor. It is assumed that much of the economy was controlled by but a few and therefore great stress was placed on the necessity to care for those in need.

Both wealth and poverty were extreme in Biblical Israel since there were no middle classes between the wealthy and the poor. Jerusalem was the center of Hebrew learning, and the residence of the priestly aristocracy who were the wealthy merchants and landlords and whose wealth was built upon the laborers and the peasants.

Slavery was commonplace in the Near East, but there was little or no slavery in Israel because Hebrew sentiment was opposed to the enslavement of one Hebrew by another. Since the Bible and the rabbis praised the dignity of manual labor, the fact that a man earned his living by working was not a social stigma. Not only Jesus and Paul, but many of the great rabbis practiced a trade; and they were accepted in the homes of the great because of their knowledge of the law.

The economic system of the Hebrews in Biblical days was agrarian since nearly all the people lived upon the land, and it was the Mosaic plan that all should be equal in possessions and position.

Luke 19 condemns man for "taking up that (which he) laid not down, and reaping that (which he) did not sow."

THE BIBLICAL LAW

He that hath two coats, let him impart to him that hath none; and he that hath meat, let him do likewise. *Luke 3:11*

. . . thou takest up that thou layedst not down, and reapest that thou didst not sow.   *Luke 19:21*

. . . . I reap where I sowed not, and gather where I have not strawed.   *Matthew 25:26*

They helped everyone his neighbor; and everyone said to his brother, be of good courage.   *Isaiah 41:16*

Thou shalt not covet thy neighbor's house.   *Exodus 20:17*

As the wild ass is the lion's prey in the wilderness: so the rich eat up the poor.   *Ecclesiasticus 13:19*

. . . There is not a more wicked thing than a covetous man. . . .
                                              Ecclesiasticus 10:9

Woe unto them that join house to house, that lay field to field, till there be no place, that they may be placed alone in the midst of the earth.   *Isaiah 5:8*

The life of him that dependeth on another man's table is not to be counted for a life; for he polluteth himself with other men's meat. . . .   *Ecclesiasticus 40:29*

. . . eat ye every one of his vine, and every one of his fig tree, and drink ye every one the waters of his own cistern.
                                                  Isaiah 36:16

. . . in all things I have kept myself from being burdensome unto you, and so will I keep myself.   *2 Corinthians 11:9*

He that tilleth his land shall have plenty of bread. . . .
                                                 Proverbs 28:19

For thou shall eat the labor of thine hands: happy shall thou be, and it shall be well with thee. *Psalms 128:2*

. . . to be content with that a man hath, is a sweet life. *Ecclesiasticus 40:18*

For we brought nothing into this world, and it is certain we can carry nothing out. And having food and raiment let us be therewith content. *1 Timothy 6:7, 8*

He that loveth gold shall not be justified . . . Gold hath been the ruin of many, and . . . it is a stumbling block unto them that sacrifice unto it. . . . *Ecclesiasticus 31:5, 6, 7*

For I [Christ] say unto you, That unto every one which hath shall be given; and from him that hath not, even that he hath shall be taken away from him. *Luke 19:26*

And he [Christ] went into the temple, and began to cast out them that sold therein, and them that bought; Saying unto them, It is written, My house is the house of prayer: but ye have made it a den of thieves. *Luke 19:45, 46*

EDUCATION

THROUGHOUT the Bible there is repetitive direction to educate the young, to learn the words of knowledge, and not only to receive instruction, but to hear counsel. To absorb wisdom, to get understanding, and that the mind should be filled with pleasures and riches, resulting only from education and learning. The Mosaic law does caution that wisdom is much grief and that a man who has great knowledge increaseth sorrow.

Biblical law directs that children shall receive their instruction from the father. There is no record of a school system. Each family taught their children the laws, and it was the head of the family who was charged with the responsibility of educating the children so that in due time they might take the place of the parents as heads of the family.

The Levites, who assisted the priests administering to the religious needs of Israel, were not required to attend a school, but were educated by their family elders in the knowledge of the requirements of their special position.

"Receive my instruction, and not silver; and knowledge rather than choice gold" is sufficient to show the high plane on which education was placed, and the importance of its acquisition.

Mandatory school attendance for children has made the United States the leader in education and progress.

THE BIBLICAL LAW

Apply thine heart unto instruction, and thine ears to the words of knowledge. *Proverbs 23:12*

Receive my instruction, and not silver; and knowledge rather than choice gold. *Proverbs 8:10*

Hear counsel, and receive instruction, that thou mayest be wise in thy latter end. *Proverbs 19:20*

Wisdom is the principal thing; therefore get wisdom; and with all thy getting get understanding. *Proverbs 4:7*

. . . The Lord is a God of knowledge. *1 Samuel 2:3*

And by knowledge shall the chambers of the mind be filled with all precious and pleasant riches. *Proverbs 24:4*

. . . that the soul be without knowledge . . . is not good. *Proverbs 19:2*

. . . a man of understanding walketh uprightly. *Proverbs 15:21*

. . . gather instruction from thy youth up: so shalt thou find wisdom till thine old age. *Ecclesiasticus 6:18*

For in much wisdom is much grief: and he that increaseth knowledge increaseth sorrow. *Ecclesiastes 1:18*

. . . be admonished; of making many books there is no end; and much study is a weariness of the flesh. *Ecclesiastes 12:12*

Thy wisdom and thy knowledge, it hath perverted thee; and thou hast said in thine heart, I am, and none else beside me. *Isaiah 47:10*

Hast thou children? Instruct them, and bow down their neck from their youth. *Ecclesiasticus 7:23*

My son, hear the instruction of thy father, and foresake not the law of thy mother. *Proverbs 1:8*

Hear, ye children, the instruction of a father, and attend to know understanding. *Proverbs 4:1*

Oh that my words . . . were printed in a book! *Job 19:23*
. . . of making books there is no end; and much study is a weariness of the flesh. *Ecclesiastes 12:12*

EMBEZZLEMENT, FRAUD
AND DECEIT

THE BIBLE likens the man who deceiveth his neighbor, to a mad man. Our laws prohibit deceitful dealing and taking advantage of another. Penalties are fixed for every deceitful act. One who obtains the promise of another by fraud is estopped from receiving any gain.

The law requires honest dealing, and that one who enters into an agreement with his fellow man must do so justly and honestly.

Embezzlement today is a statutory crime, and there must be proof of the taking of some specific property mentioned in the statute.

It is difficult to compare Biblical sins with statutory crimes since in the former all are based on moral and spiritual values whereas in the latter only that is a crime which fits into the structure of the statute sought to be enforced.

Man's desire to have the possessions of others has been the subject of much legal legislation. Gaining property, whether real or personal, by fraud and deceit has been a curse of man from time immemorial.

The Mosaic law condemns deceit, fraud, and all unrighteous dealings between men. Centuries have changed many things, but man's greed is still the subject of our punitive legal system.

THE BIBLICAL LAW

If a soul . . . lie unto his neighbor in that which was delivered
him to keep, or in a thing taken away by violence, or hath
deceived his neighbor . . . or have found that which was lost,
and lieth concerning it, and sweareth falsely . . . then . . . he
shall restore that which he took violently away, or the thing
which he hath deceitfully gotten, or that which was delivered
him to keep, or the lost thing which he found . . . or all that
about which he has sworn falsely; he shall restore it in the
principal, and shall add a fifth part more thereto. . . .

Leviticus 6:1, 2, 3, 4, 5

The getting of treasures by a lying tongue is a vanity. . . .

Proverbs 20:6

. . . defraud not. . . .   *Mark 10:19*

Defraud ye not one another. . . .   *1 Corinthians 7:5*

. . . we have wronged no man, we have corrupted no man, we
have defrauded no man.   *2 Corinthians 7:2*

For ye know what commandments we gave you . . . that no
man go beyond and defraud his brother in any matter. . . .

1 Thessalonians 4:2, 6

. . . he that getteth riches, and not by right, shall leave them
in the midst of his days and at his end shall be a fool.

Jeremiah 17:11

Thou shalt not defraud thy neighbor. . . .

Leviticus 19:13

He that worketh deceit shall not dwell within my house. . . .

Psalms 101:7

EVIDENCE AND WITNESSES

IN THE CONDUCT of a trial each litigant is required to produce evidence to prove his claim, or to disprove the claim of his opposition. The history of evidence has from the beginning put the burden on him who contends for his position and he is required to prove his case by producing his evidence first. He must bring forth his witnesses who must give honest and truthful evidence of the facts, known to them of their own knowledge, or they may relate that which they have seen, and under some circumstances and conditions, that which they have heard.

Each witness must testify concerning actual facts and not what he thinks or infers. It is for the judge, or the jury to resolve the testimony given, and to conclude which is or is not to be believed.

Mosaic law did not require, as today, that before a witness testified in a court of law, he take an oath before God to tell the truth. Through the ages some form of oath-taking has been mandatory before a witness could be heard. Since in our practice no inquiry is made of the person taking such oath as to his belief in God or his belief in immortality, or his belief in punishment after death, in the event he has sworn falsely, it seems useless to administer an oath to one who disregards its moral as well as legal obligation.

The giving of testimony, and the taking of evidence from witnesses, is one of the most important events in man's juridical systems.

When testimony is being given by an honest witness who testifies to something he saw, he represents under oath that he accurately saw or heard some past events; that now he accurately remembers what he saw or heard; and that he is now accurately reporting his memory. Into each of these three, error can enter, and often does. Observation is not a mechanical process. While part of what man perceives comes from the object before him, another part—and it may be the greater part—always comes out of his mind.

A reading of Ruth 4:7 indicates that evidence of sale and purchase, and perhaps evidence of the completion of any transaction, was by manual and physical acts: "Now this was the manner in former time in Israel concerning redeeming and concerning changing, for to confirm all things; a man plucked off his shoe, and gave it to his neighbor: and this was testimony in Israel."

What is meant by "now this was the manner in former time in Israel" is not clear. It can mean that this "manner" of evidence was the existing rule, or it may be the statement of an earlier custom. However, when read together with all that precedes and follows the above quotation it is safe to assume that reference is made to an existing rule of evidence.

Cross-Examination

Two chapters of the Book of Daniel appear only in the Apocrypha because neither was written in Hebrew. Had they been in Hebrew they would have been Chapters 13 and 14 of Daniel.

The second of these chapters is the history of the Destruction of Bel and the Dragon. It deals with Daniel in the lions' den. The other is called The History of Susanna, and treats of Daniel's defense of a woman accused of adultery and against whom there were two witnesses who testified they saw her in the act. She was, as a result, sentenced to death. Daniel, in effect, asked that a new trial be granted her. This was done and Daniel, acting as defense counsel, cross-examined the two accusers and established the falsity of their testimony. The book closes with the punishment decreed for the two perjurers: "And they arose against the two elders (for Daniel had convicted them of false witness by their own mouth) and according to the law of Moses they did unto them in such sort as they maliciously intended to do their neighbor: and they put them to death."

Trial

There was no manner of jury trial known to the Mosaic law. The procedure was for the judges who tried the case to examine all witnesses and afterward in their deliberations to first advance all the arguments available in favor of the defense. Their opening argument or discussion must be for acquittal. It is from this Mosaic principle that we have inherited the legal premise that all men are presumed to be innocent, and cannot be convicted until the contrary is proved to a moral certainty and beyond a reasonable doubt.

Self-Incrimination

In our law the privilege against self-incrimination doubtless had its birth in the abhorrence with which confessions coerced by inquisitorial means were regarded by all men. The rule is that no defendant in a criminal case may be compelled to be a witness against himself.

The accused was never compelled to testify against himself. A confession of guilt was accepted in evidence and considered in connection with other facts of the case, but standing alone it could not be the basis of a conviction. Maimonides in his commentaries on the Mishna discusses this rule: "We have it as a fundamental principle of our jurisprudence that no one can bring an accusation against himself. Should a man make a confession of guilt before a legally constituted tribunal, such confession is not to be used against him, unless properly attested by two other witnesses. It is, however, well to remark that the death sentence issued against Achan (Joshua 7:19, 20, 24, 25) was an exceptional case, brought about by the nature of the circumstances attending it, for our law never condemns on the single confession of an accused part."

During the military leadership of Joshua, self-incrimination was an accepted legal procedure as more fully appears in the biblical description of the case of Achan.

Circumstantial Evidence

Only direct evidence was permitted under biblical law. The strongest chain of circumstantial evidence would not suffice for conviction. Witnesses were instructed that hearsay evidence was not admissible. The witness, to testify in a trial, must give evidence only of that which he actually heard or had seen. As directed in Deuteronomy 17:6 "at the mouth of two witnesses, or three witnesses, shall he that is worthy of death be put to death."

Most of the procedural rules are found only in the Mishna and the Gemara, which are books of the decisions construing the Mosaic law.

Qualification of Witnesses

Women, because of the "levity and boldness of the sex" were not permitted to testify. This was particularly true in capital cases, since the law required the witness to be the executioner.

Minors were competent witnesses if passed their thirteenth birthday.

Those who were "wicked", or those known as immoral or irreligious people were not accepted as witnesses.

In the list of incompetent witnesses there is included: slaves, idiots, deaf mutes, lunatics, gamblers, blind men, usurers, the immodest, and the illiterate.

All witnesses presented in a case were required to agree in all essential details. If one contradicted another in any material matter, their entire testimony was disregarded. This rule applied in criminal cases only; it was not the rule in civil cases.

It was mandatory that witnesses give their testimony separately, but always in the presence of defendant.

Pretrial and Discovery Proceedings

Our law has but recently adopted a pretrial and discovery procedure intended to limit the issues and facts in each case, and to discard immaterial or irrelevant evidence. Our procedure contemplates a hearing before the judge prior to the scheduled trial to simplify the issues in controversy, and avoid unnecessary proof of facts. The Biblical law provided for, and used this procedure thousands of years ago.

To prevent the admission of irrelevant testimony, a preliminary examination of witnesses was conducted in private by a committee of the members of the Sanhedrin. All irrelevant testimony developed at this private examination was cast aside. The result of this proceeding was the discovery of discrepancies in statements of witnesses. The full court sitting in regular session was not, therefore, exposed to or prejudiced by facts that had no legal connection with the case, since every impression, legal or illegal, received at a trial, affects the judgment of the court or jury and enters into the resulting verdict.

THE BIBLICAL LAW

Thou shalt not bear false witness against thy neighbor.
Exodus 20:16

For a man's mind is sometime want to tell him more than seven watchmen, that sit above in an high tower.
Ecclesiasticus 37:14

And Joshua said unto Achan . . . make confession . . . and tell me now what thou has done: and Achan . . . said, Indeed I have sinned . . . and thus and thus have I done. And Joshua and all Israel took Achan . . . and his sons and his daughters . . . and all that he had . . . and all Israel stoned him . . . and burned them with fire. . . .   *Joshua 7:19, 20, 24, 25*

Let them bring them forth, and shew us what shall happen: let them show the former things, what they be, that we may consider them, and know the latter end of them; or declare us things for to come.   *Isaiah 41:22*

. . . Let them bring forth their witnesses, that they may be justified: or let them hear, and say, It is truth. *Isaiah 43:9*

A faithful witness will not lie: but a false witness will utter lies.   *Proverbs 14:5*

. . . one witness shall not testify against any person to cause him to die.   *Numbers 35:30*

One witness shall not rise up against a man for any iniquity, or for any sin that he sinneth: at the mouth of two witnesses, or at the mouth of three witnesses, shall the matter be established.
Deuteronomy 20:15

. . . Thy blood be upon thy head; for thy mouth hath testified against thee. . . .   *2 Samuel 1:16*

The hands of the witnesses shall be first upon him to put him to death, and afterward the hands of all the people.
Deuteronomy 17:7

Be not a witness against thy neighbor without cause. . . .
Proverbs 24:28

Do not bear false witness against thy neighbor. *Exodus 20:16*

For children begotten of unlawful beds are witnesses of wicked-ness against their parents in their trial. *Wisdom of Solomon 4:6*

Thine own mouth condemneth thee, and not I. Yea, thine own lips testify aaginst thee.
Job 15:6

If I justify myself, mine own mouth shall condemn me. . . .
Job 9:20

For by thy words thou shalt be justified, and by thy words thou shalt be condemned.
Matthew 12:37

Blame not before thou hast examined the truth: understand first, and then rebuke.
Ecclesiasticus 11:7

Answer not before thou hast heard the cause: neither in-terrupt men in the midst of their talk. *Ecclesiasticus 11:8*

FOOD

"THERE IS nothing better for a man, than that he should eat and drink, and that he should make his soul enjoy good in his labor." However, by Biblical law man was cautioned to use discretion and moderation and to be temperate in all eating and drinking. Ecclesiasticus cautions that man "should have a care of his meat and diet."

While the Bible says that every man that strives for mastery is temperate in all things it also provides that no one "be unsatiable in any dainty thing, nor too greedy upon meats" and that "excess of meats bringeth sickness, and surfeiting will turn into choler. By surfeiting many have perished; but he that taketh heed prolongeth his life."

Leviticus II and Deuteronomy 14 contain the laws and directives concerning the foods which may be eaten. Each animal, fowl, and fish is "clean" which may be eaten, or "unclean" which may not be eaten.

Prohibition prevails against eating anything with blood, and that one shall "pour it upon the ground as water."

Table manners too are given consideration, and suggestions for man's conduct when visiting and dining are suggested. It may be assumed that the culture of Biblical times demanded a high degree of decorum and decent conduct. That proper etiquette is discussed is evidence of a life of social amenities and that all life was not herding of sheep and tilling of fields.

THE BIBLICAL LAW

Let your moderation be known unto all men.
Philippians 4:5

Sound sleep cometh of moderate eating: he riseth early, and his wits are with him. *Ecclesiasticus 31:20*

. . . temperance: against such there is no law.
Galatians 5:23

There is nothing better for a man, than that he should eat and drink, and that he should make his soul enjoy good in his labor. *Ecclesiastes 2:24*

. . . every man should eat and drink, and enjoy the good of his labor. . . . *Ecclesiastes 3:13*

. . . it is good and comely for one to eat and to drink and to enjoy the good of all his labor that he taketh under the sun all the days of his life. *Ecclesiastes 5:18*

A cheerful and good heart will have a care of his meat and diet. *Ecclesiasticus 30:25*

Be not unsatiable in any dainty thing, nor too greedy upon meats. *Ecclesiasticus 37:29*

For excess of meats bringeth sickness, and surfeiting will turn into choler. *Ecclesiasticus 37:30*

By surfeiting many have perished; but he that taketh heed prolongeth his life. *Ecclesiasticus 37:31*

And every man that striveth for the mastery is temperate in all things. *1 Corinthians 9:25*

. . . of every tree of the garden thou mayest freely eat; but of the tree of knowledge of good and evil, thou shalt not eat of it. . . . *Genesis 2:16, 17*

It is good neither to eat flesh, nor to drink wine, nor anything whereby thy brother stumbleth, or is offended or is made weak.

Romans 14:21

Every moving thing that liveth shall be meat for you; even as the green herb. . . .

Genesis 9:3

Thou shalt not eat any abominable thing. *Deuteronomy 14:3*

. . . These are the beasts which ye shall eat among all the beasts that are on the earth. Whatever parteth the hoof and is clovenfooted, and cheweth the cud . . . nevertheless these shall ye not eat of them that chew the cud, or of them that divide the hoof; as a camel, because he cheweth the cud, but divideth not the hoof; he is unclean unto you.   *Leviticus 11:2, 3, 4*

Ye shall not eat of anything that dieth of itself. . . .

Deuteronomy 14:21

. . . neither shall ye eat any flesh that is torn of beasts in the field; ye shall cast it to the dogs.   *Exodus 22:31*

. . . ye shall eat no manner of blood, whether it be of fowl or of beast. . . .   *Leviticus 7:26*

Ye shall not eat anything with the blood. . . .

Leviticus 19:26

And whatever man there be of the House of Israel, or of the strangers that soujourn among you that eateth any manner of blood; . . . cut him off from his people. *Leviticus 17:10*

No soul of you shall eat blood, neither shall any stranger that sojourneth among you eat blood.   *Leviticus 17:12*

Ye shall eat the blood of no manner of flesh; for the life of all flesh is the blood thereof. . . .   *Leviticus 17:14*

Ye shall eat no manner of fat, of ox, or of sheep or of goat.

Leviticus 7:23

It shall be a perpetual statute for your generations throughout all your dwellings, that ye eat neither fat nor blood.

Leviticus 3:17

GENERAL LAWS

CONSIDERATION IS GIVEN the many laws and statutes proclaimed in the Bible dealing with general conditions affecting the every day living of the Hebrew people.

The routine of living then was not much different than it is today. Prohibition against man wearing women's clothing and juvenile delinquency receive attention. Equality before the law, begging, kidnapping, mortgages, insane persons, and all forms of general subjects arising in community living are provided for. It is clear in Biblical history that life in the cities and on the farms required regulation as much then as it does today.

Interesting comparisons can be made. For cleanliness, man was required to cut his hair short. This was necessary in a country of heat, sand, and where the supply of water was limited.

Much of the law in the Bible is the law today, and which our legislatures enact and repeat and re-enact from time to time. Could we but transfer ourselves from our street to a street in the Holy Land as it existed then, it seems there would be little difference insofar as the laws are concerned.

The many Biblical laws for the treatment of indigents and the poor generally, indicate the great poverty of the lower classes. Whether this was due to the economy of the Holy Land or to the caste system is not clear.

THE BIBLICAL LAW

Application of Laws

One law shall be to him that is homeborn, and unto the stranger that sojourneth among you. *Exodus 12:49*

. . . he [the King] shall write him a copy of this law in a book out of that which is before the priests . . . and he shall read therein . . . that he may learn . . . to keep all the words of this law and these statutes, to do them.
Deuteronomy 17:18, 19

A wise man hateth not the law . . . a man of understanding trusteth in the law; and the law is faithful unto him. . . .
Ecclesiasticus 33:2, 3

It is easier for heaven and earth to pass, than one tittle of the law to fail. *Luke 16:17*

Where no law is, there is no transgression. *Romans 4:15*

. . . the law is not made for a righteous man, but for the lawless and disobedient. *1 Timothy 1:8, 9*

Avoid . . . strivings about the law; for they are unprofitable and vain. *Titus 3:9*

Bastards

A bastard shall not enter unto the congregation of the Lord; even to his tenth generation shall he not enter into the congregation of the Lord. *Deuteronomy 23:2*

Begging

Be not a beggar by banqueting upon borrowing, when thou hast nothing in thy purse. . . . *Ecclesiasticus 18:33*

. . . lead not a begger's life: for better it is to die than to beg. The life of him that dependeth on another man's table is not to be counted for a life; for he polluteth himself with other men's meat. *Ecclesiasticus 40:28*

Better is the life of a poor man in a mean cottage, than delicate fare in another man's house. *Ecclesiasticus 29:22*

Birds and Bees

If a bird's nest chance to be before thee . . . in any tree or on the ground, whether they be young ones, or eggs, and the dam setting upon the young, or upon the eggs, thou shalt not take the dam with the young. But thou shalt in any wise let the dam go, and take the young to thee. . . .
Deuteronomy 22:6, 7

The bee is little among such as fly; but her fruit is the chief of sweet things. *Ecclesiasticus 11:3*

Building Code

For which of you, intending to build a tower, sitteth not down first, and counteth the cost, whether he have sufficient to finish it? *Luke 14:28*

When thou buildest a new house, then thou shalt make a battlement for thy roof, that thou bring not blood upon thy house, if any man fall from thence. *Deuteronomy 22:8*

He that buildeth his house with other men's money is like one that gathereth himself stones for the tomb of his burial.
Ecclesiasticus 21:8

Clothes

The woman shall not wear that which pertaineth unto a man, neither shall a man put on a woman's garment: for all that do so are abomination. . . . *Deuteronomy 22:5*

Thou shalt not wear a garment of a divers sorts, as of woolen and linen together.   *Deuteronomy 22:11*

Diet

Ye shall eat no manner of fat, or ox, or of sheep, or of goat.
                                                      Leviticus 7:23

Equality Before the Law

One law shall be to him that is homeborn, and unto the stranger that sojourneth among you.   *Exodus 12:49*

Flight

The wicked flee when no man pursueth: but the righteous are bold as a lion.   *Proverbs 28:1*

Fortune-Tellers and Magicians

Ye shall not . . . use enchantment, nor observe times.
                                                     Leviticus 19:26

Regard not them that have familiar spirits, neither seek after wizards, to be defiled by them.   *Leviticus 19:31*

Divinations, and soothsayings, and dreams, are vain: for dreams have deceived many, and they have failed that put their trust in them.   *Ecclesiasticus 34:5, 7*

And when they say unto you, Seek unto them that have familiar spirits, and unto wizards that peep, and that mutter: should not a people seek unto their God?   *Isaiah 8:19*

And the soul that turneth after such as have familiar spiritis, and after wizards, to go a whoring after them . . . I will cut him off from among his people.   *Leviticus 20:6*

There shall not be found among you anyone that maketh his son or his daughter to pass through the fire, or that useth divination, or an observer of times, or an enchanter, or a witch, or a charmer, or a consulter with familiar spirits, or a wizard, or a necromancer.   *Deuteronomy 18:10, 11*

Gambling

And Aaron . . . shall take . . . two goats . . . and shall cast lots upon the two goats; one lot for the Lord, and the other lot for the scapegoat . . . to let him go for a scapegoat unto the wilderness. . . .   *Leviticus 16:7, 8, 9, 10*

. . . the land shall be divided by lot. . . .   *Numbers 26:55*

The lot causes contentions to cease. . . .   *Proverbs 18:18*

Guests

. . . I opened my doors to the traveller.   *Job 31:32*

Bring not every man unto thine house: for the deceitful man hath many trains (paths).   *Ecclesiasticus 11:29*

Who will trust a thief . . . that skippeth from city to city? so [who will believe] a man that hath no house, and lodgeth wheresoever the night taketh him?   *Ecclesiasticus 36:26*

. . . howsoever let all thy wants lie upon me; only lodge not in the street.   *Judges 19:20*

If any . . . bid you to a feast, and ye be disposed to go, whatsoever is set before you, eat, asking no questions.
                                   1 Corinthians 10:27

Hair

. . . If a man have long hair, it is a shame unto him, but if a woman have long hair, it is a glory to her. . . .
                                   1 Corinthians 11: 14, 15

Indigents

Give alms of thy substance; and when thou givest alms, let not thine eye be envious, neither turn thy face from any poor. . . .
Tobit 4:7

If thou hast abundance, give alms accordingly; if thou have but a little, be not afraid to give accordingly to that little.
Tobit 4:8

. . . relieve the oppressed. . . .   *Isaiah 1:17*

Strengthen ye the weak hands, and confirm the feeble knees.
Isaiah 35:3

Rob not the poor, because he is poor: neither oppress the afflicted. . . .   *Proverbs 22: 22*

. . . Go and bring the poor, and the maimed, and the halt, and the blind.   *Luke 14:21*

Thou shalt not curse the deaf, nor put a stumbling block before the blind. . . .   *Leviticus 19:14*

Cursed be he that maketh the blind to wander out of the way.
Deuteronomy 27:18

Dishonor not a man in his old age: even some of us wax old.
Ecclesiasticus 8:6

Rebuke not an elder, but intreat him as a father . . . the elder women as mothers. . . .   *1 Timothy 5:1, 2*

Thou shalt open thine hand wide unto thy brother, to thy poor, to thy needy, in thy land.   *Deuteronomy 15:11*

And when ye reap the harvest of your land, thou shalt not make clean riddance of the corners of thy field when thou reapest; neither shalt thou gather any gleaning of thy harvest: thou shalt leave them unto the poor, and to the stranger. . . .
Leviticus 23:22

For the poor shall never cease out of the land. . . .

Deuteronomy 15:11

Thou shalt rise up before the hoary head, and honor the face of the old man. *Leviticus 19:32*

That the aged man be sober, grave, temperate, sound in faith, in charity, in patience. The aged woman likewise, that they be in behavior as becometh holiness, not false accusers, not given to much wine, teachers of good things. *Titus 2:2, 3*

For the poor shall never cease out of the land: therefore I command thee, saying Thou shalt open thine hand wide unto thy brother, to thy poor, and to thy needy. . . .

Deuteronomy 15:11

And oppress not the widow, nor the fatherless, the stranger, nor the poor. . . . *Zechariah 7:10*

Blessed is he that considereth the poor. *Psalms 41:1*
And if thy brother be waxen poor, and fallen in decay with thee; then thou shalt relieve him: yea, though he be a stranger, or a sojourner; that he may live with thee. *Leviticus 25:35*

. . . thou . . . shalt surely lend him sufficient for his need . . .

Deuteronomy 15:8

And if thy brother that dwelleth by thee be waxen poor, and be sold unto thee; thou shalt not compel him to serve as a bond-servant: but as an hired servant, and as a sojourner, he shall be with thee . . . and then shall he depart from thee, both he and his children with him. . . . *Leviticus 25:39, 40, 41*

I have been young, and now am old; yet have I not seen the righteous forsaken, nor his seed begging bread. *Psalms 37:25*

. . . if any would not work, neither should he eat.

2 Thesalonians 3:10

. . . when ye reap the harvest of your land, thou shalt not wholly reap the corners of thy field . . . and thou shalt not . . . gather every grape of thy vineyard; thou shalt leave them for the poor and stranger. . . . *Leviticus 19:9, 10*

When thou cuttest down thine harvest in thy field, and hast forgot a shief in the field, thou shalt not go again to fetch it . . . When thou beatest thine olive tree, thou shalt not go over the boughs again, and it shall be for the stranger, for the fatherless, and for the widow.   *Deuteronomy 24:19, 20*

Be as a father unto the fatherless, and instead of an husband unto their mother. . . .   *Ecclesiasticus 4:10*

Ye shall not afflict any widow, or fatherless child.
                                                 Exodus 22: 22

Insane Persons

. . . have mercy on my son: for he is a lunatic, and sore vexed. . . .   *Matthew 17:15*

. . . comfort the feebleminded, support the weak, be patient to all men.   *1 Thessalonians 5:14*

Juvenile Delinquency

Do not sin against the child. . . .   *Genesis 42:22*

If a man have a stubborn and rebelious son, which will not obey the voice of his father, or the voice of his mother, and that, when they have chastened him, will not hearken unto them . . . [then] all the men of the city shall stone him with stones, that he die.   *Deuteronomy 21:18, 19, 20, 21*

Chasten thy son while there is hope, and let not thy soul spare for his crying.   *Proverbs 19:18*

Withhold not correction from the child: for if thou beatest him with the rod, he shall not die.   *Proverbs 23:13*

Hast thou children? instruct them, and bow down their neck from their youth.   *Ecclesiasticus 7:23*

Children, obey your parents in all things: for this is well pleasing to the Lord.   *Colossians 3:20*

An horse not broken becometh headstrong: and a child left to himself will be wilful.   *Ecclesiasticus 30:8*

Knowledge of the Law

At the end of every seven years, in the solemnity of the year of release, thou shalt read this law before all Israel in their hearing. Gather the people, together, men and women, and children, and thy stranger that is within thy gates, that they may hear and that they may learn . . . and observe to do all the words of this law.   *Deuteronomy 31:10-12*

Thou shalt teach them (The Commandments) dilligently unto thy children, and shalt talk of them when thou sittest in thine house and when thy walkest by the way, and when thy liest down, and when risest up . . . and thou shalt write them upon the posts of thy house, and on thy gates.
                                              Deuteronomy 6:7-9

Lost or Found Property

Thou shalt not see thy brother's ox or his sheep go astray . . . thou shalt in any case bring them again unto thy brother. And if thy brother be no nigh unto thee, or if thou know him not, then thou shalt bring it unto thine own house, and it shall be with thee until thy brother seek after it, and thou shalt restore it to him again . . . and with all lost things of thy brother's, which he has lost and thou hast found, shalt thou do likewise; thou mayest not hide thyself.
                                            Deuteronomy 22:1, 2, 3

If a soul . . . have found that which was lost and lieth concerning it, and sweareth falsely . . . he shall restore . . . the lost thing which he found . . . and shall add the fifth part more thereto.   *Leviticus 6:25*

Mourning and Burial

Seven days do men mourn for him that is dead. . . .
                                            Ecclesiasticus 22:12

. . . let tears fall down over the dead, and begin to lament, as if thou hadst suffered great harm thyself; and then cover his body according to the custom, and neglect not his burial.

Ecclesiasticus 38:15

Mortgages

. . . We have mortgaged our lands, vineyards, and houses, so that we might buy corn. . . . *Nehemiah 5:3*

Offenses Against the Person

If men strive and hurt a woman with child, so that her fruit depart from her, and yet no mischief follow . . . he shall pay as the judges determine. *Exodus 21:22*

And if any mischief follow, then thou shalt give life for life. Eye for eye, tooth for tooth, hand for hand, foot for foot.

Exodus 21:23, 24

And if a man cause a blemish in his neighbor; as he has done, so shall it be done to him. *Leviticus 24:19*

When men strive together one with another, and the wife of the one draweth near for to deliver her husband out of the hand of him that smiteth him, and putteth forth her hand and taketh him by the secrets: then thou shalt cut off her hand. . . .

Deuteronomy 25:11, 12

Removing Landmarks

Thou shalt not remove thy neighbor's landmarks, which they of old time have set. *Deuteronomy 19:14*

Cursed be he that removeth his neighbor's landmark.

Deuteronomy 27:17

Remove not the ancient landmark, which thy fathers have set.

Proverbs 22:28

Social Behavior

If thou sit at a bountiful table, be not greedy upon it, and say not, there is much meat on it. *Ecclesiasticus 31:12*

Eat as it becometh a man, those things which are set before before thee; and devour not, lest thou be hated.
Ecclesiasticus 31:16

Leave off first for manners' sake; and be not unsatiable, lest thou offend. *Ecclesiasticus 31:17*

The greater thou art, the more humble thyself. . . .
Ecclesiasticus 3:18

Some man holdeth his tongue, because he hath not to answer: and some keepeth silence, knowing his time.
Ecclesiasticus 20:6

Let your speech be always with grace, seasoned with salt, that ye may know how ye ought to answer every man.
Colossians 4:6

Without eyes thou shalt want light: profess not the knowledge therefore that thou hast not. *Ecclesiasticus 3:25*

He that hath no experience knoweth little. . . .
Ecclesiasticus 34:10

When thou sittest among many, reach not thine hand out first of all. *Ecclesiasticus 31:18*

A very little is sufficient for a man well nurtured, and he fetcheth not his wind short . . . sound sleep cometh of moderate eating. . . . *Ecclesiasticus 31:19, 20*

For the wages of sin is death. . . . *Romans 6:23*

[He] loved the wages of unrighteousness. *2 Peter 2:15*
If any of them that believe not bid you to a feast, and ye be disposed to go; whatsoever is set before you, eat, asking no question for conscience sake. *1 Corinthians 10:27*

, . . him that hath an high look and a proud heart will not I suffer. *Psalms 101:5*

Put not forth thyself . . . and stand not in the place of great men. For better it is that it be said unto thee, come up hither; then that thou shouldest be put lower. . . . *Proverbs 25:6, 7*

Swearing

Thou shalt not take the name of the Lord thy God in vain. . . . *Exodus 20:7*

And ye shall not swear by my name falsely. *Leviticus 19:12*

Use not thy mouth to intemperate swearing, for therein is the word of sin. *Ecclesiasticus 23:13*

But I say unto you, swear not at all. . . . *Matthew 5:34*

. . . swear not, neither by heaven, neither by the earth, neither by any other oath. . . . *James 5:12*

The talk of him that sweareth much maketh the hair stand upright. . . . *Ecclesiasticus 27:14*

Tatooing

. . . [do not] print any marks upon you. . . . *Leviticus 19:28*

Widows and Orphans Pensions

Then the high priest told him that there was . . . money laid up for the relief of widows and fatherless children. *2 Maccabees 3:10*

Ye shall not afflict any widow, or fatherless child. If thou afflict them in any wise, and they cry at all unto me . . . I will kill you with the sword; and your wives shall be widows and your children fatherless. *Exodus 22:22, 23, 24*

Witchcraft

And I will cut off witchcrafts out of thine hand; and thou shalt have no more soothsayers. *Micah 5:12*

A man also or a woman that hath a familiar spirit, or that is a wizard, shall surely be put to death: they shall stone them.
Leviticus 20:27

Thou shalt not suffer a witch to live. *Exodus 22:18*

GIFTS

A GIFT is a transfer of property, made voluntarily and without consideration. In order for a gift to be valid, there must be a complete delivery and transfer of dominion within the donor's lifetime. Acceptance by the donee is an essential element of a completed gift. To create a valid and enforceable gift there must be a donative intent by the donor, an effectual transfer of title and delivery, and an actual or imputed acceptance by the donee. A clear intention on the part of the donor to make a gift is essential to a valid gift and it is sufficient if the donor uses words clearly importing an intention to give.

The Bible understands man: "every one loveth gifts, and followeth after rewards."

THE BIBLICAL LAW

. . . it is more blessed to give than to receive. *Acts 20:35*

. . . let him labor, working with his hands . . . that he may have to give him that needeth. *Ephesians 5:28*

And thou shalt take no gift: for the gift blindeth the wise, and perverteth the words of the righteous. *Exodus 23:8*

He that is greedy of gain troubleth his own house; but he that hateth gifts shall live. *Proverbs 15:27*

Unto the sons of the (his) concubines . . . Abraham gave gifts . . . and sent them away. . . . *Genesis 25:6*

Take, I pray thee, my blessing (gift) that is brought to thee; because God hath dealt graciously with me, and because I have enough . . . *Genesis 33:11*

. . . a gift destroyeth the heart (understanding). *Ecclesiastes 7:7*

. . . and he that giveth to the rich, shall surely come to want. *Proverbs 22:16*

Give to him that asketh thee, and from him that would borrow of thee turn not thou away. *Matthew 5:42*

. . . sell whatever thou hast, and give to the poor . . . *Mark 10:21*

. . . Say not unto thy neighbor, Go, and come again, and tomorrow I will give; when thou hast it by thee. *Proverbs 3:28*

. . . Give unto the good and help not the sinner. *Ecclesiasticus 12:7*

Give not thy son and wife, thy brother and friend, power over thee while thou livest, and give not thy goods to another: lest it repent thee, and though intreat for the same again.
As long as thou livest and hast breath in thee, give not thyself over to any. *Ecclesiasticus 33:19, 20*

GOVERNMENT AND CRIMES
AGAINST THE STATE

AFTER THE RETURN from Babylonian captivity, the influence of the priesthood so grew that when, for a period under the Maccabees, the Hebrews won their political liberty, both spiritual and temporal power were in its hands. The Mosaic institutions, too, received several additions: writers, many of them laymen, devoted to the study and explanation of the law, and the Sanhedrin or council of elders, which, during the Greek domination was the chief administrative authority.

The duties of the priests were not confined to religious matters. They were the governing class, and performed political functions. Provisions for their support took the place of taxes.

The priesthood was a distinct hereditary order, and while priests might marry women of non-priestly families, they had to be undefiled virgins or widows of pure Israelite extraction. The high-priest might marry only an undefiled Israelite virgin.

The Levites, like the priests, were a hereditary order and were entrusted with duties such as singers, janitors, servants of the priests, and the carrying on of the menial conduct of the temple and the work performed by the priests.

The separation of church and state is a modern development. In ancient states and communities, the priest was not only the king, but also the judge. This government of and by priests is known as theocracy, but Constantine the Great adopted the principle that the church was subservient to the state, and so it is to this day.

THE BIBLICAL LAW

When the righteous are in authority, the people rejoice; but when the wicked beareth rule, the people mourn.

Proverbs 29:2

. . . He that ruleth over men must be just, ruling in the fear of God. *11 Samuel 23:3*

Thou shalt in any wise set him King over thee, whom the Lord thy God shall choose; one from among thy brethren shalt thou set king over thee: thou mayest not set a stranger over thee, which is not thy brother. *Deuteronomy 17:15*

Woe to thee, O land, when thy King is a child . . .

Ecclesiastes 10:16

O King of Judah . . . execute ye judgment and righteousness, and deliver the spoiled out of the hand of the oppressor: and do no wrong, do no violence to the stranger, the fatherless, nor the widow, neither shed innocent blood. . . .

Jeremiah 22:3

. . . and my princes shall no more oppress my people. . . .

Ezekiel 45:8

Thou shalt not . . . curse the ruler of thy people.

Exodus 22:28

Obey them that hath rule over you, and submit yourselves . . .

Hebrews 13:17

Moreover thou shalt provide . . . men of truth . . . to be rulers of thousands, and rulers of hundreds, rulers of fifties, and rulers of tens. *Exodus 18:21*

. . . what manner of man the ruler of the city is, such are all they that dwell therein. *Ecclesiasticus 10:2*

. . . proclaim liberty throughout all the land unto all the inhabitants thereof. *Leviticus 25:10*

[Do not use] your liberty for a cloak of maliciousness.

1 Peter 2:16

Breach of the Peace

. . . seek peace and pursue it. *Psalms 34:14*

. . . but that thou thyself also walkest orderly, and keepest the law. *Acts 21:24*

And be at peace among yourselves. *1 Thessalonians 5:13*
Let us therefore follow after the things which make for peace . . . *Romans 14:19*

If it be possible, as much as lieth in you, live peaceably with all men. *Romans 12:18*

Abstain from strife . . . for a furious man will kindle strife.

Ecclesiasticus 28:8

Strive not with a man without cause, if he hath done thee no harm. *Proverbs 3:30*

Strive not in a matter that concerneth thee not . . .

Ecclesiasticus 11:9

Thou shalt not follow a multitude to do evil . . .

Exodus 23:2

Petty Treason

And he that smiteth his father, or his mother, shall be surely put to death. *Exodus 21:15*

Rumor Mongers

Thou shalt not raise a false report . . . *Exodus 23:1*

Thou shalt not go up and down as a talebearer among thy people . . . *Leviticus 19:16*

A talebearer revealeth secrets: but he that is of a faithful spirit concealeth the matter. *Proverbs 11:13*

Rehearse not unto another that which is told unto thee. . . .
Ecclesiasticus 19:7

Be not a whisperer, and lie not in wait with thy tongue. . . .
Ecclesiasticus 5:14

These . . . things doth the Lord hate . . . he that soweth discord among brethren. *Proverbs 6:16, 19*

Treason

Whosoever . . . doth rebel against thy commandment, and will not hearken unto thy words in all that thou commandest him, he shall be put to death . . . *Joshua 1:18*

And the man that will do presumptuously, and will not harken . . . unto the judge, even that man shall die.
Deuteronomy 17:12

Then Athaliah rent her clothes, and cried, Treason, Treason.
2 Chronicles 23:13

. . . bow down your shoulders to serve the King of Babylon: so shall ye remain in the land that I gave unto your fathers.
2 Baruch 2:21

I counsel thee to keep the king's commandment . . .
Ecclesiastes 8:2

We will not hearken to the king's words, to go from our religion, either on the right hand, or the left.
1 Maccabees 2:22

HEALTH

THE REPUBLIC of Venice established the first Board of Health. It consisted of three nobles, and was called the "Council of Health." It was ordered to investigate the best means of preserving health, and of preventing the introduction of disease from abroad. Its efforts not having been entirely successful, its powers were enlarged in 1504, so as to grant it "the power of life and death over those who violated the regulations for health." No appeal was allowed from the sentence of this tribunal.

During the plague in London in 1665, the magistrates consulted to devise means for stopping, or at least impeding, the progress of the disease, and the result of their deliberations was a series of orders which appointed commissioners, searchers, and buriers to each district. Every house which was visited, as it was called, was by those orders marked with a red cross of a foot long in the middle of the door, evident to be seen.

Under Biblical law, health regulations were administered and enforced by the priests, who were thus the forerunners of modern health officers and boards of health.

The Mosaic law also required personal cleanliness as well as moral and spiritual cleanliness. The Bible provides for the isolation and segregation of the diseased and for their being quarantined particularly where communicable diseases are involved.

THE BIBLICAL LAW

Better is the poor, being sound and strong of constitution, than a rich man that is afflicted in his body. Health and good estate of body are above all gold, and a strong body above infinite wealth.   *Ecclesiasticus 30:14, 15*

There is no riches above a sound body, and no joy above the joy of heart.   *Ecclesiasticus 30:16*

Death is better than a bitter life or continual sickness.
                    Ecclesiasticus 30:17

Beloved, I wish above all things thou mayest . . . be in health.
                    3 John 2

Woe unto you . . . Hypocrites! For ye make clean the outside of the cup and of the platter, but within they are full of extortion and excess.   *Matthew 23:25*

O Jerusalem, wash thine heart . . .   *Jeremiah 4:14*
. . . let us cleanse ourselves from all filthiness of the flesh . . .
                    2 Corinthians 7:1

And when they come from the market, except they wash, they eat not.   *Mark 7:4*

And if any man's seed of copulation go out from him, then he shall wash all his flesh in water . . .   *Leviticus 15:16*

The woman also with whom a man shall lie with seed of copulation, they shall both bathe themselves in water . . .
                    Leviticus 15:18

Be not overmuch wicked, neither be thou foolish: why shouldest thou die before thy time?   *Ecclesiastes 7:17*

The days of our years are threescore years and ten.
                    Psalms 90:10

Quarantine

Command the children of Israel, that they put out of the camp every leper, and every one that hath an issue . . .

Numbers 5:2

All the days wherein the plague shall be in him . . . he shall dwell alone; without the camp shall his habitation be.

Leviticus 13:46

He shall therefore burn that garment, whether warp or woof, in woolen or in linen, or anything of skin, wherein the plague is . . .

Leviticus 13:52

HOMICIDE

HOMICIDE is either felonious, excusable or justifiable.

The law arms every private citizen in the community with the power of life and death for the prevention of atrocious felonies accompanied with violence and personal danger to others, as in case of an attempt to murder or rob, or commit burglary or arson, the person making the attempt may, if he cannot be otherwise prevented, be killed on the spot, and the law will not recognize the act as a crime. In cases of this sort, in order to justify the homicide, it must appear that there were good grounds for a suspicion that the person killed has a felonious intent. A woman is justifiable in killing one who attempts to ravish her, and the husband or father may be justified in killing a man who attempts a rape on his wife or daughter.

The cases of justifiable homicide are those in which the public authority and laws are directly concerned. The laws of society, however, leave every individual a portion of that right of personal defense with which he is invested by nature. As one may interpose to prevent an atrocious crime against society, where he is not himself in any personal danger, the laws will permit him to defend himself against attacks upon his own person.

Murder is the killing of a person with malice aforethought, either express or implied. It is not necessary in order to constitute the crime of murder that the slayer should have the direct intention of killing. If the act be done with a wicked, depraved, malignant spirit, a heart regardless of social duty, and deliberately bent upon mischief it is characterized by what the law denominates malice though it may not result from any enmity or grudge against the particular victim. So if a man wantonly discharges a gun among a group of people, whereby any one is killed, the act will be done with that depravity of disposition which the law considers malice.

Murder can be committed only by a free agent, for the crime presupposed a will, or disposition on the part of the perpetrator. An idiot or insane person cannot commit this crime, and drunkenness is in general no excuse for homicide, though the act be done under its immediate influence.

The manner of killing is not material. Whether it be by shooting, poison, beating, imprisonment, starvation or exposure to the inclemency of the atmosphere, it will be equally murder. This crime may be committed by mere advice and encouragement.

The lines of distinction between felonious and excusable or justifiable homicide, and between manslaughter and murder, are in many cases difficult to define with precision. The characteristic distinction between murder and manslaughter is the absence of malice in the latter. Sudden provocation may be an excuse for striking another without the intention to give a deadly blow; and though death ensue, the party may not be guilty of murder. One circumstance, showing the degree of malice, or rather showing its presence or absence, is the kind of weapon used in giving a wound on a sudden provocation; and another circumstance of importance is the fact of the weapon's being already in the hand or not, for going to seek a weapon gives time for deliberation. The ground of excuse for homicide, in case of provocation merely, is the supposed sudden passion, some influence of which the law concedes to the frailty of human nature. But the excuse of self-defense goes still further; and where a man is attacked, so that his own life is endangered, or in such way that he may reasonably suppose it to be so, he may repel the attack with mortal weapons.

The crime of murder in its most aggravated degree is punished with death in most parts of the civilized world.

THE BIBLICAL LAW

Thou shalt not commit murder. (Hebrew Version)

Exodus 20:13

Thou shalt not kill. (Protestant and Catholic Version)

Exodus 20:13

Whose sheddeth man's blood, by man shall his blood be shed.

Genesis 9:6

. . . Thou shalt do no murder . . .   *Matthew 19:18*

. . . the innocent and righteous slay thou not . . .

Exodus 23:7

Cursed be he that taketh reward to slay an innocent person.

Deuteronomy 27:25

And he that killeth any man shall surely be put to death.

Leviticus 24:17

He that smiteth a man so that he die, shall be surely put
to death.   *Exodus 21:12*

And if a man lie not in wait, but God deliver him (the victim)
unto his hand; then I will appoint thee a place whither he shall
flee. But if a man come presumptuously upon his neighbor to
slay with guile; thou shalt take him from mine alter, that he
may die.   *Exodus 21:13, 14*

If a thief be found breaking up, and be smitten that he die,
there shall no blood be shed from him. If the sun be risen
upon him there shall be blood shed for him; for he should
make full restitution: if he have nothing, then he shall be sold
for his theft.   *Exodus 22:2, 3*

. . . blood . . . defileth the land: and the land cannot be
cleansed of the blood that is shed therein, but by the blood of
him that shed it.   *Numbers 35:33*

. . . when wicked men have slain a righteous person in his
own house upon his bed, shall I not therefore now require
his blood of your hand? . . .   *2 Samuel 4:11*

HUSBAND AND WIFE

THE FAMILY is the most important element in human society, and the destruction of the family would destroy the state and nation. The primitive family was an independent unit and the simplest form of society. The oldest male was ordinarily the Chief and was the law. As man progressed from the single family unit to tribal groups, and then nations, laws replaced the directives of the family heads. Most of these general laws were directed toward and defined the relationship of husband and wife.

It is the duty of husband and wife to adhere to the marriage contract and cohabit; the husband having the right to determine the place of domicile. If he changes the same the wife must go with him; though there are times when the husband is obliged to show a reasonable cause for removing to another abide in order to obligate the wife to follow him. The unreasonable refusal of the wife to follow would be an act of desertion. There is a duty that the spouses by mutual forbearance make living together tolerable. The Common Law of England would find few supporters today. It provided that a husband may correct his wife by subjecting her to restraint and even to "moderate" corporeal punishment. Such restraint and chastisement would have to be very moderate to satisfy modern ideas of ethical or legal propriety.

If the husband drives his wife from his house by "conduct so abominable that no decent woman would live under the same roof with him," her departure would not be desertion. Incontinence, of course, would justify the innocent party in leaving the guilty one, and no legal right would be forfeited in consequence.

The duty of the husband to protect implies his right to defend the wife from personal injury; and a battery committed by either in defense of the other is justifiable and lawful.

The husband must support and maintain the wife as long as she lives with him. He is not relieved from this duty even though the wife have independent means adequate to her needs. The obligation of the husband is to provide "necessaries", and to obtain these the wife may contract debts which the husband, by law, is bound to pay.

When husband and wife are living together there is a presumption that the wife has the husband's authority to enter into contracts, binding on the latter, in relation to all domestic matters ordinarily entrusted to the woman of the house, and to obtain on the husband's credit the things necessary to the conduct of the household. The term "necessaries" means a reasonable supply of such goods and services as are suitable in kind, sufficient in quantity and required in fact, for the use of the husband, the wife, the children and other members of the household, according to the conditions in which they live

Marriage is considered a sacred obligation, but in most nations it is created by a civil contract regulated by law. Polygamy is not prohibited by the Bible and Biblical law provides no punishment. It was an accepted institution and depended on the economic ability of the man to provide for his wives. Polygamy was practiced in ancient Israel and until outlawed, in the State of Utah.

Shakespeare in the Taming of the Shrew (Act 3, Scene

2) has Petruchio restate the Biblical relation of husband and wife: "I will be master of what is my own: she is my goods, my chattels; she is my house, my household stuff, my field, my barn, my horse, my ox, my ass, my anything." The wife was the property of her husband.

THE BIBLICAL LAW

Thou shalt not commit adultery. *Exodus 20:14*

Therefore shall a man leave his father and his mother, and shall cleave unto his wife: and they shall be one flesh.
Genesis 2:24

For the husband is the head of the wife . . .
Ephesians 5:23

And God blessed them (Adam and Eve), and God said . . . be fruitful and multiply . . . *Genesis 1:28*

Take ye wives, and beget sons and daughters; and take wives for your sons, and give your daughters to husbands, that they may bear sons and daughters . . . *Jeremiah 29:6*

Lo, children are a heritage of the Lord and the fruit of the womb is his reward. *Psalms 127:3*

. . . every man should bear rule in his own house . . .
Esther 1:22

Hast thou a wife after thy own mind? Foresake her not: but give not thyself over to a light woman. *Ecclesiasticus 7:26*

Husbands, love your wives . . . let every one of you in particular so love his wife even as himself. *Ephesians 5:33*

Likewise, ye husbands, dwell with them (wives) according to knowledge, giving honor unto the wife, as unto the weaker vessel . . . *1 Peter 3:7*

Wives, submit yourselves unto your own husbands . . .
Colossians 3:18

Husbands, love your wives, be not bitter against them.
Colossians 3:19

Let the husband render unto the wife due benevolence: and likewise also the wife unto the husband.   *1 Corinthians 7:3*

Be not jealous over the wife of thy bosom, and teach her not an evil lesson against thyself.   *Ecclesiasticus 9:1*

But if any provide not for his own, and specially for those of his own house, he hath denied the faith, and is worse than an infidel.   *1 Timothy 5:8*

. . . teach the young women to be sober, to love their husbands, to love their children, to be discreet, chaste, keepers (workers) at home, good, obedient to their husbands.

Titus 2:4, 5

. . . the wives shall give to their husbands honor, both to great and small.   *Esther 1:20*

An honest woman will reverence her husband.

Ecclesiasticus 26:24

. . . women . . . are commanded to be under obedience . . .

1 Corinthians 14:34

Who can find a virtuous woman? . . . The heart of her husband doth safely trust in her . . . She will do him good and not evil . . .   *Proverbs 31:10, 11, 12*

. . . she that is married careth . . . how she may please her husband . . .   *1 Corinthians 7:34*

. . . Thou shalt not covet thy neighbor's wife . . .

Exodus 20:17

. . . thy desire shall be to thy husband, and he shall rule over thee.   *Genesis 3:16*

A virtuous woman is a crown to her husband . . .

Proverbs 12:4

An evil wife is a yoke shaken to and fro: he that hath hold of her is as though he held a scorpion.   *Ecclesiasticus 26:7*

Desire not a multitude of unprofitable children, neither delight in ungodly sons.   *Ecclesiasticus 16:1*

. . . let them marry to whom they think best; only to the family of the tribe of their father shall they marry.
                                                 Numbers 36:6

. . . to avoid fornication, let every man have his own wife, and let every woman have her own husband.
                                            1 Corinthians 7:1, 2

I say . . . to the unmarried and widows, it is good for them if they abide even as I. But if they cannot contain, let them marry: for it is better to marry than to burn.
                                            1 Corinthians 7:8, 9

The wife is bound by the law as long as her husband liveth; but if her husband be dead, she is at liberty to be married to whom she will . . .   *1 Corinthians 7:39*

If brethren dwell together, and one of them die, and have no child, the wife of the dead shall not marry without unto a stranger: her husband's brother shall go unto her, and take her to him to wife and perform the duty of a husband's brother unto her. And it shall be, that the firstborn which she beareth him shall succeed in the name of his brother which is dead, that his name be not put out of Israel. *Deuteronomy 25:5, 6*

Ask me never so much dowry and gift, and I will give according as ye shall say unto me: but give me the damsel to wife.
                                                 Genesis 34:12

A wise daughter shall bring an inheritance (dowry) to her husband . . .   *Ecclesiasticus 22:4*

And Boaz said unto the elders and unto all the people, Ye are witnesses this day, that . . . Ruth the Moabitess . . . have I purchased to be my wife . . . and all the people . . . and the elders . . . said, we are witnesses. So Boaz took Ruth, and she was his wife.   *Ruth 4:9, 10, 11, 13*

Then he called his daughter, Sara, and she came to her father, and he . . . gave her to be wife to Tobias . . . and called Edna his wife, and took paper and did write an instrument of covenants, and sealed it. *Tobit 7:13, 14*

When a man hath taken a new wife, he shall not go out to war, neither shall he be charged with any business: but he shall be free at home one year, and shall cheer up his wife which he has taken. *Deuteronomy 24:5*

Rejoice with the wife of thy youth. *Proverbs 5:18*

Live joyfully with the wife whom thou lovest all the days of life of thy vanity . . . for that is thy portion in this life.
Ecclesiastes 9:9

Let every one of you . . . love his wife even as himself.
Ephesians 5:33

A man shall leave his father and his mother, and shall cleave unto his wife: and they shall be one flesh. *Genesis 2:24*

. . . let every man have his own wife, and let every woman have her own husband. *1 Corinthians 7:2*

Let the husband render unto the wife due benevolence: and likewise also the wife unto the husband. *1 Corinthians 7:3*

A bishop then must be . . . the husband of one wife . . . Even so must their wives be grave, not slanderers, sober, faithful in all things. *1 Timothy 3:2, 11*

They (the priests) shall not take a wife, that is a wrote, or profane; neither shall they take a woman put away from her husband . . . *Leviticus 21:7*

A widow, or a divorced woman, or profane (godless) or an harlot, these shall he (the priests) not take: but he shall take a virgin of his own people to wife. *Leviticus 21:14*

Neither shalt thou make marriages with them (foreigners); thy daughter thou shalt not give unto his son, nor his daughter shalt thou take unto thy son. *Deuteronomy 7:3*

. . . take a wife of the seed of thy fathers, and take not a
strange woman to wife, which is not of thy father's tribe.

Tobit 4:12

A silent and loving woman is a gift of the Lord . . .

Ecclesiasticus 26:14

LABOR

In Biblical times, as today, manual labor was an honorable calling. It was not unusual for the worker to be educated in the law and to sit with the wealthy in discussion of the Mosaic writings.

Labor laws have been part of every judicial system in history, and since early in the twentieth century the working man has been protected by legislation to guarantee him equality of living conditions and opportunities for education and advancement.

In modern industry brains are needed as well as muscle. Men are educated and trained to do jobs that were in the last century thought fit for only the unlearned. Organized productive forces depend upon the ability quite as much as upon the skill and strength of the manual worker.

The economic system of the Bible is based on the fact that nearly all of Israel lived upon the land. Every man was directed to "eat the labor of thine hands and happy shalt thou be."

The unwillingness to work and to live by means other than by honest effort is condemned: "Go to the ant thou sluggard; consider her ways, and be wise: which having no guide, overseer or ruler, provideth her meat in the summer, and gathereth her food in the harvest. How long wilt thou sleep, a little slumber, a little folding of the hands to sleep: so shall thy poverty come as one that travelleth, and thy want as an armed man." This advice in 6 Proverbs may be the forerunner of our laws against idle loiterers and those who wander around without occupation or visible means of support.

Dignity of man, liberty of the individual, and freedom from oppression are all basic in Mosaic jurisprudence. Liberty in its broad sense is the right, not only of freedom from actual servitude, but the right of one to use his faculties in all lawful ways, to live, to work and to earn a livelihood in any lawful manner.

The matter of retirement age was of concern in Biblical days as now. The Mosaic law in reference to the Levites fixes the term of years to be worked before retirement: "from twenty and five years old and upward they (the Levites) shalt go in to wait upon the service of the Tabernacle of the congregation; and from the age of fifty years they shall cease waiting upon the service thereof, and shall serve no more: but shall minister with their brethren in the Tabernacle of the congregation, to keep the charge, and shall do no service." While 8 Numbers fixes this rule as to the Levites, there is no general law in the Mosaic code covering length of service or retirement.

Deuteronomy prohibits unfair dealing with labor: "thou shalt not oppress an hired servant that is poor and needy, whether he be of thy brethren, or of thy strangers," and "at his day thou shalt give him his hire." And Jeremiah "woe unto him that useth his neighbor's service without wages, and giveth him not for his work."

All was not perfect, and relation between employer and employee was not always satisfactory to both sides in Biblical days. As today, wage and hour disputes arose:
. . . an householder, which went out early in the morn-

ing to hire laborers unto his vineyard . . . he agreed with the laborers for a penny a day . . . and about the eleventh hour he went out, and found others (laborers) and said to them, go ye also into the vineyard; and whatever is right, that shall ye receive. So when even was come . . . they received every man a penny. But when the first came, they supposed that they should have received more; and they likewise received every man a penny . . . they murmured . . . saying, these last have wrought but one hour, and thou hast made them equal unto us, which have borne the burden and heat of the day. But he answered . . . and said friend, I do thee no wrong: didst thou not agree with me for a penny? Take that thine is, and go thy way. . . . *Matthew 20:1, 2, 7, 8, 9, 10, 11, 12, 13, 14*

The soul of the sluggard desireth, and hath nothing . . .

Proverbs 13:4

Whatsoever thy hand findeth to do, do it with thy might.

Ecclesiastes 9:10

In all labor there is profit   *Proverbs 14:23*

Better is he that laboreth, and aboundeth in all things, than he that boasteth himself, and wanteth bread.

Ecclesiastes 10:27

The sluggard will not plow by reasons of the cold; therefore shall he begin harvest, and have nothing.   *Proverbs 20:4*

Go to the ant thou sluggard; consider her ways and be wise: which having no guide, overseer, or ruler, provideth her meat in the summer, and gathereth her food in the harvest. How long wilt thou sleep, O sluggard? When wilt thou arise . . . ?

Proverbs 6:6, 7, 8, 9

In the sweat of thy face shalt thou eat bread . . .

Genesis 3:19

But let every man prove his own work, and then shall he have rejoicing in himself alone . . . For every man shall bear his own burden.   *Galatians 6:4, 5*

. . . that with quietness they work, and eat their own bread.

2 Thessalonians 3:12

Let him who stole steal no more: but rather let him labor, working with his hands . . .   *Ephesians 4:28*

To labor, and to be content with that a man hath, is a sweet life . . .   *Ecclesiasticus 40:18*

He that tilleth his land shall have plenty of bread . . .

Proverbs 28:19

. . . thou shalt eat the labor of thine hands: happy shalt thou be, and it shall be well with thee.   *Psalms 128:2*

. . . every man should eat and drink, and enjoy the good of all his labor . . .   *Ecclesiastes 3:13*

The husbandman that laboreth must be first partaker of the fruits.   *2 Timothy 2:6*

For we brought nothing into this world, and it is certain we can carry nothing out. And having food and raiment let us be therewith content.   *Timothy 6:7, 8*

Do violence to no man, neither accuse any falsely; and be content with your wages.   *Luke 3:14*

Hate not laborious work . . .   *Ecclesiasticus 7:15*

He that laboreth, laboreth for himself; for his mouth craveth it of him.   *Proverbs 16:26*

The hand of the diligent shall bear rule: but the slothful shall be under tribute.   *Proverbs 12:24*

. . . if any would not work, neither should he eat.

2 Thessalonians 3:10

. . . an idle soul shall suffer hunger.   *Proverbs 18:15*

I therefore . . . beseech you that ye walk worthy of the vocation wherewith ye are called.   *Ephesians 4:1*

. . . we have done that which was our duty to do.

Luke 17:10

And Pharoah's daughter said unto her, take this child away, and nurse it for me, and I will give thee thy wages . . .

Exodus 2:9

. . . and he rested on the seventh day from all his work . . .
Genesis 2:2

Six days may work be done; but in the seventh is the sabbath of rest . . . *Exodus 31:15*

Six days shalt thou labor, and do all thy work . . .
Exodus 20:9

Thou hypocrite, doth not each one of you on the sabbath loose his ox . . . from the stall, and lead him to watering?
Luke 13:15

Thou shalt not oppress an hired servant that is poor and needy, whether he be of thy brethren, or of thy strangers that are in thy land within thy gates. *Deuteronomy 24:14*

. . . every man shall receive his own reward according to his own labor. , *1 Corinthians 3:8*

. . . he that defraudeth the laborer of his hire is a blood-shedder. *Ecclesiasticus 34:22*

Woe unto him . . . that useth his neighbor's service without wages, and giveth him not for his work. *Jeremiah 22:13*

. . . the laborer is worthy of his hire. *Luke 10:7*

. . . the laborer is worthy of his reward. *1 Timothy 5:18*

Now to him that worketh is the reward not reckoned of grace, but of debt. *Romans 4:4*

. . . the recompense of a man's hands shall be rendered unto him. *Proverbs 12:14*

Let not the wages of any man, which hath wrought for thee, tarry with thee, but give him it out of hand . . . *Tobit 4:14*

. . . the wages of him that is hired shall not abide with thee all night until the morning. *Leviticus 19:13*

At his day thou shalt give him his hire, neither shall the sun go down upon it; for he is poor, and sitteth his heart upon it . . .

Deuteronomy 24:15

Woe unto him that buildeth his house by unrighteousness, and his chambers by wrong; that useth his neighbor's service without wages, and giveth him not for his work.

Jeremiah 22:13

. . . and he that earneth wages earneth wages to put it into a bag with holes. *Haggai 1:6*

. . . Thou shalt not covet . . . thy neighbor's man-servant, nor his maidservant . . . *Exodus 20:17*

Because thou art my brother, shouldst thou therefore serve me for naught? Tell me, what shall thy wages be? *Genesis 29:15*

A laboring man that is given to drunkenness shall not be rich . . . *Ecclesiasticus 19:1*

LAW, LAWYERS AND JUDGES

LAWYERS were unknown to the Mosaic judicial system. The judges who tried the accused were also his defenders. In such legal system lawyers were unnecessary, and in the early Biblical days, litigants pleaded their own cases, as appears in the case of the two women who appeared before King Solomon, and argued their respective claims to a child (I Kings 3:16-28). Not until the New Testament is there mention of lawyers.

There was no accusatory body such as our Grand Jury. The witnesses were the accusers; their testimony constituting both the indictment and the evidence.

There was no attorney general, district attorney or state prosecutor. In capital cases the witnesses were not only the prosecutors, and givers of evidence, but executioners as well.

The highest court in Israel was the Sanhedrin. This Aramaic word Sanhedrin is identical with the Greek synedrion; assembly or council. When this institution arose cannot be definitely determined, but from the earliest times local government had been conducted by a council of the elders, men whose age, rank and wealth gave weight to their decisions. It is possible that it was established by Moses in the wilderness in accordance with the command in Numbers 11:16, 17: "Gather unto me seventy men . . . whom thou knowest to be the elders of the people . . . and bring them unto the tabernacle of the congregation, that they may stand there with thee. And I will come down and talk with thee there . . . and they shall bear the burden of the people with thee, that thou bear it not thyself alone."

The presidency of the Sanhedrin was vested in the high-priest, who was the supreme magistrate. The original composition of the Sanhedrin was exclusively aristocratic: members of the high-priestly families, and the 'elders' of the lay aristocracy. At one period scribes were admitted. These classes are the 'chief priests, elders and scribes' of the Gospels.

No court could consist of a single judge. There were three courts which were charged with the trial of cases; the Great Sanhedrin, seventy-one judges; the Minor Sanhedrin, twenty-three; the Lower Tribunal, or the Court of Three. The Great Sanhedrin sat in Jerusalem. It had original jurisdiction of all offenses committed by those in public office, and of offenses affecting the security of the country.

The jurisdiction of the Sanhedrin was originally very broad, including all religious questions, and all civil and criminal cases. It was the supreme authority in determining the interpretation of the law, both oral and written. It had its own police force.

The Criminal Procedure of the Sanhedrin favored the accused. In capital cases, the arguments of the defense were heard first, and favorable testimony was irreversible. Unfavorable testimony could be reversed. It was mandatory that a delay of one day intervene between the trial and sentence. A majority of one sufficed for acquittal; a majority of two was required for conviction.

According to the Mishna, a guilty vote by thirty-seven of the seventy-one members of the Sanhedrin was needed to convict. The procedure in Biblical trial law provided that a unanimous verdict of guilty rendered on the day of trial, had the effect of an acquittal. Such unanimous verdict was thought to result more from a group hatred conspiracy rather than from mature deliberation.

The study and interpretation of the law was in the hands of those who are called scribes and doctors of law in the Gospels. Originally the interpretation of the Torah (law) was the function of the priests; but the scribes as such were not priests, although priests were included in their number. Once the Law was accepted as the basis of Hebrew life, it was necessary to determine its meaning, and to apply it, as far as possible, to situations that might arise. Hence, the scribes. The name is first given to Esdras, 'a ready scribe in the law of Moses.'

The scribes had no official position; and their opinions had no authority except that of personal influence and public opinion. But this authority was enough. They were legislators, teachers and judges. They sat 'in the chair of Moses,' and were addressed by the title of Rabbi (master). The study of the law was, in the eyes of the devout, the highest occupation. It was not remunerative; many of the scribes, who did not enjoy an independent income, were quite poor and supported themselves by a trade.

THE BIBLICAL LAW

And he [Christ] said, Woe unto you also, ye lawyers! for ye lade men with burdens grievous to be borne, and ye yourselves touch not the burdens with one of your fingers. *Luke 11:46*

. . . neither shalt thou speak in a cause to decline after many to wrest judgment. *Exodus 23:2*

Thou shalt not wrest the judgment of thy poor in his cause. *Exodus 23:6*

Thou shalt not pervert the judgment of the stranger, nor of the fatherless; nor take a widow's raiment to pledge. *Deuteronomy 24:17*

I charge thee . . . that thou observe these things without prefering one before another, doing nothing by partiality. *1 Timothy 5:21*

Then stood there up one in the council . . . a doctor of the law, had in reputation among all the people, and commanded to put the apostles forth . . . and said . . . take heed to yourselves what ye intend to do as touching these men. *Acts 5:34, 35*

The one of them, which was a lawyer asked him a question . . . saying Master which is the best commandment in the law? *Matthew 22:35, 36*

But the Pharisees and lawyers rejected the counsel of God . . . *Luke 7:30*

Judges and officers shalt thou make . . . throughout thy tribes: and they shall judge the people with just judgment. *Deuteronomy 16:18*

Thou shalt not wrest judgment; thou shalt not respect persons, neither take a gift: for a gift doth blind the eyes of the wise, and pervert the words of the righteous. *Deuteronomy 16:19*

If one man sin against another, the judge shall judge him. . . .
1 Samuel 2:25

Many seek the ruler's favor; but every man's judgment cometh from the Lord. *Proverbs 29:26*

Mercy is seasonable in the time of affliction, as clouds of rain in the time of drought. *Ecclesiasticus 35:20*

And Moses chose able men out of all Israel . . . and they judged the people at all season; the hard causes they brought unto Moses, but every small matter they judged themselves.
Exodus 18:25, 26

Thus saith the Lord . . . do justice. *Isaiah 56:1*

And thou, Ezra . . . set magistrates and judges, which may judge all the people that are beyond the river, all such as know the laws . . . and teach ye them that know them not. *Ezra 7:25*

Judge not that ye be not judged. *Matthew 7:1*

For with what judgment ye judge, ye shall be judged: and with what measure ye mete, it shall be measured to you again.
Matthew 7:2

. . . and he (Moses) said to him that did the wrong, wherefore smitest thou thy fellow? And he said, who made thee a judge over us? . . . *Exodus 2:13, 14*

And he (Samuel) went from year to year in circuit to Beth-el and Gilgal, and Mizpeh, and judged Israel in all those places. And his return was to Ramah; for there was his house; and there he judged Israel. . . . *1 Samuel 7:16, 17*

A man of understanding trusteth in the law; and the law is faithful unto him. . . . *Ecclesiasticus 33:3*

And I (Moses) charged your judges . . . saying, Hear the causes between your brethren, and judge righteously between every man and his brother, and the stranger that is with him.
Deuteronomy 1:16

Ye shall not respect persons in judgment; but ye shall hear the small as well as the great; ye shall not be afraid of the face of man . . . and the cause that is too hard for you, bring it unto me, and I will hear it.   *Deuteronomy 1:17*

Ye shall do no unrighteousness in judgment; thou shalt not respect the person of the poor, nor honour the person of the mighty: but in righteousness shalt thou judge thy neighbor.
                              Leviticus 19:15

And he (Jehosphaphat, King of Judah) set judges in the land throughout all the fenced cities of Judah . . . and said to the judges, take heed what ye do: for ye judge not for man, but for the Lord, who is with you in judgment.
                           2 Chronicles 19:5, 6

And what cause soever shall come to you for your brethren . . . . between blood and blood, between law and commandment, statutes and judgments, ye shall even warn them that they trespass not against the Lord . . . *2 Chronicles 19:10*

Ye shall do no unrighteousness in judgment . . .
                              Leviticus 19:35

Woe unto them that decree unrighteous decrees, and that write grievousness which they have prescribed; to turn aside the needy from judgment, and to take away the right from the poor of my people . . .   *Isaiah 10:1, 2*

Absolom said moreover, Oh that I were made judge in the land, that every man which hath any suit or cause might come unto me, and I would do him justice!   *2 Samuel 15:4*

He (the King) shall judge thy people with righteousness, and thy poor with judgment.   *Psalms 72:2*

. . . execute the judgment of truth and peace in your gates (courts) .   *Zechariah 8:16*

Judge not according to the appearance, but judge righteous judgment.   *John 7:24*

Then said Pilate unto them, Take ye him (Christ) and judge him according to your law. The Jews therefore said unto him, it is not lawful for us to put any man to death. *John 18:31*

And in controversy they shall stand in judgment; and they shall judge it according to my judgments.   *Ezekiel 44:24*

If there be a controversy between men, and they come unto judgment, that the judges may judge them; then they shall justify the righteous and condemn the wicked.
Deuteronomy 25:1

How long will ye judge unjustly, and accept the persons of the wicked? . . . Defend the poor and fatherless: do justice to the afflicted and needy.   *Psalms 82:2, 3*

For this is a heinous crime; yea, it is an iniquity, to be punished by the judges.   *Job 31:11*

And the judges shall make diligent inquisition: and, behold, if the witness be a false witness, and hath testified falsely against his brother; then shall ye do unto him, as he had thought to have done unto his brother . . .   *Deuteronomy 19:18, 19*

Love righteousness, ye that be judges of the earth . . .
Wisdom of Solomon 1:1

A wise judge will instruct his people . . . *Ecclesiasticus 10:1*

. . . be not fainthearted when thou sittest in judgment.
Ecclesiasticus 4:9

For all manner of trespass, whether it be for ox, for ass, for sheep, for raiment, or for any manner of lost thing, which another challengeth to be his, the cause of both parties shall come before the judges; and whom the judges shall condemn, he shall pay double unto his neighbor.   *Exodus 22:9*

So shall I keep thy law continually forever and ever. And I will walk at liberty: for I seek thy precepts. *Psalms 119:44, 45*

. . . where the spirit of the Lord is, there is liberty.
2 Corinthians 3:17

But we know that the law is good, if a man use it lawfully.
1 Timothy 1:8

. . . the law is not made for a righteous man, but for the lawless and disobedient . . . *1 Timothy 1:9*

Let thy tender mercies come unto me, that I may live: for thy law is my delight. *Psalms 119:77*

I hate and abhor lying: but thy law do I love.
Psalms 119:163

Now we know that what things soever the law saith, it saith to them who are under the law . . . *Romans 3:19*

But whoso looketh into the perfect law of liberty, and continueth therein . . . shall be blessed in his deed. *James 1:25*

Then spake Jesus . . . saying . . . all therefore whatsoever they bid you observe, that observe and do. *Matthew 23:1, 2, 3*

Submit yourselves to every ordinance of man for the Lord's sake: whether it be of the King . . . or unto governors, as unto them that are sent by him for the punishment of evildoers . . . *1 Peter 2:13, 14*

And he said unto them, Render therefore unto Caeser the things which be Caeser's, and unto God the things which be God's. *Luke 20:25*

Law Suits

Go not to law with a judge; for they will judge for him according to his honor. *Ecclesiasticus 8:14*

. . . he that undertaketh and followeth other men's business for gain shall fall into suits. *Ecclesiasticus 29:19*

And if a man will sue thee at the law, and take away thy coat, let him have thy cloke also. *Matthew 5:40*

But we know that the law is good, if a man use it lawfully.
1 Timothy 1:8

Moreover if thy brother shall trespass against thee, go and tell him his fault between thee and him alone . . . But if he will not hear thee . . . tell it unto the church.
Matthew 18:15, 16, 17

Dare any of you, having a matter against another, go to law . . . it is so, that there is not a wise man among you? No, not one that shall be able to judge between his brethren?
1 Corinthians 6:1, 5

. . . If thy brother trespass against thee, rebuke him; and if he repent, forgive him. And if he trespass against thee seven times in a day, and seven times in a day turn again to thee, saying, I repent; thou shalt forgive him.   *Luke 17:3, 4*

Appeals

And they (the judges) judged the people at all season: the hard causes they brought unto Moses, but every small matter they judged themselves.   *Exodus 18:26*

If there arise a matter too hard for thee in judgment . . . then shalt thou . . . come unto the priests the Levites, and unto the judge that shall be in those days, and enquire; and they shall show thee the sentence of judgment . . . and according to the judgment . . . thou shalt do . . . thou shalt not decline . . . to the right hand, nor to the left.
Deuteronomy 17:8, 9, 10, 11

LIBEL AND SLANDER

SLANDER in general is the defaming of a man in his reputation by speaking words from whence any injury to his character or property arises, or may arise. It is generally limited in the legal sense to defamation by words spoken, and which words tend to the prejudice of the reputation, office, trade, business, or means of getting a living. This definition is subject to many legal changes and additions, and is used only to establish the general subject as it pertains to Biblical law.

The various books of the bible deal with the prohibition against slander, and is indicative of the existence of much social intercourse among the wandering Hebrew tribes. Then as now a man's reputation was a valuable asset and was protected by law.

Today as in biblical times the utterance of defamatory words injuring another's reputation or suggesting that he has an "evil disease" is slander.

Defamation of persons or property is actionable by either criminal or civil process.

Libel as known in our law today, is not mentioned as such in the Bible. Alexander Hamilton defined libel as a censorious or ridiculing writing, picture, or sign, made with malicious intent towards individuals. Since biblical and general history indicates that only a few knew how to read and write, it is not strange that Mosaic law should not mention libel.

Set a watch, O Lord, before my mouth; and a door round about my lips.
Psalms 141:3

An hypocrite with his mouth destroyeth his neighbor. . . .
Proverbs 11:9

Put them in mind . . . to speak evil of no man.
Titus 3:1, 2

Let no corrupt communication proceed out of your mouth . . .
Ephesians 4:29

Speak not evil one of another . . .   *James 4:11*

If a man take a wife, and go in into her, and hate her, and give occasions of speech against her, and bring up an evil name upon her, and say, I took this woman, and when I came to her, I found her not a maid . . . the elders of that city shall take that man and chastise him; but if this thing be true . . . then . . . the men of the city shall stone her . . . that she die . . .   *Deuteronomy 22:13, 14, 18, 20, 21*

he that uttereth a slander, is a fool.   *Proverbs 10:18*

All that hate me whisper together against me . . . an evil disease say they, cleaveth fast unto him . . . *Psalms 41:7, 8*

Whoso privily slandereth his neighbor, him will I cut off. . . .
Psalms 101:5

LOANS AND PLEDGES

A LOAN is a contract wherein one party agrees to let another party have the use of a sum of money, or of a particular thing, for a definite period of time in consideration of a promise by the borrower to repay it with or without interest. It is the delivery of a sum of money to another under a contract to return it at some future time with or wihout an additional sum agreed on for its use. This contract or agreement may be expressed or it may be implied. It needs no particular form, but something must be lent, and there must be a lender and a borrower.

An important element of a loan is delivery, that is, delivery to another for use. While this does not mean a manual delivery by the lender to the borrower, it does mean a parting with the thing lent by the lender and its acquisition by the borrower. The borrower is bound to take good care of the thing borrowed, and to use it only according to the intention of the lender. It is an essential and characteristic feature of a loan that it be returnable. The borrower expressly or impliedly promises to return the thing lent. This promise to repay is absolute.

A transaction of this kind may be without reward or compensation. Ordinarily, the compensation for the use of money is called interest.

A pledge is a transfer of personal property. It can be as security for a debt, or other obligation. It is a delivery of goods by a debtor to his creditor to be kept until the debtor's obligation is discharged. It is in the form of a lien created by the owner of personal property by the mere delivery to another on an express or implied understanding that it shall be retained as security for a debt. A pledge differs from a sale; in the case of a pledge, only the possession of the property passes, and not the title thereto, while in the case of a sale, transfer of possession may or may not be made.

The philosopher of the Bible, Ecclesiasticus, sums up the general weaknesses of man concerning loans "till he hath received, he will kiss a man's hand; and for his neighbor's money he will speak submissly: but when he should repay, he will prolong the time, and return words of grief, and complaint of the time."

And if a man borrow ought of his neighbor, and it be hurt, or die, the owner thereof being not with it, he shall surely make it good. But if the owner thereof be with it, he shall not make it good: if it be an hired thing, it came for his hire.

Exodus 22:14, 15

A good man sheweth favour, and lendeth . . .

Psalms 112:5

. . . Love ye your enemies, and do good, and lend for nothing . . .   *Luke 6:35*

He that hath pity upon the poor lendeth unto the Lord; and that which he has given will he pay him again.

Proverbs 19:17

. . . and lend, hoping for nothing again. . . . *Luke 6:35*

Many, when a thing was lent them, reckoned it to be found, and put them to trouble that helped them . . . many therefore have refused to lend for other men's ill dealing, fearing to be defrauded . . . yet have thou patience with a man in poor estate, and delay not to show him mercy. *Ecclesiasticus 29:4, 7, 8*

Till he hath received, he will kiss a man's hand; and for his neighbors money he will speak submissly: but when he should repay, he will prolong the time, and return words of grief, and complain of the time.   *Ecclesiasticus 29:5*

Lend to thy neighbor in time of his need, and pay thou thy neighbor again in due season.   *Ecclesiasticus 29:2*

The wicked borroweth, and payeth not again . . .

Psalms 37:21

No man shall take the nether or the upper millstone to pledge: for he taketh a man's life to pledge.

Deuteronomy 24:6

Thou shalt not . . . take a widow's raimant to pledge.
Deuteronomy 24:17

When thou doest lend thy brother anything, thou shalt not go
unto his house to fetch his pledge. Thou shalt stand abroad, and
the man to whom thou doest lend shall bring out the pledge
abroad unto thee. And if man be poor, thou shalt not sleep
with his pledge; in any case thou shalt deliver him the pledge
again when the sun goeth down that he may sleep in his own
raiment . . .   *Deuteronomy 24:10, 11, 12, 13*

. . . he that hath not restored the pledge . . . shall surely
die . . .   *Ezekiel 18:12, 13*

Lend not unto him that is mightier than thyself; for if thou
lendest him, count it but lost.   *Ecclesiasticus 8:12*

He that is hasty to give credit is lightminded . . .
Ecclesiasticus 19:4

For the love of money is the root of all evil . . .
1 Timothy 6:10

He that buildeth his house with other men's money is like
one that gathereth himself stones for the tomb of his burial.
Ecclesiasticus 21:8

Be not made a beggar by banqueting upon borrowing, when
thou hast nothing in thy purse.   *Ecclesiasticus 18:33*

MASTER AND SERVANT

BLACKSTONE in his Commentaries on the Law points out
that there are three great relationships in private life:

1. That of master and servant; which is founded in
convenience, whereby a man is directed to call in the assistance of others, where his own skill and labor will not
be sufficient to answer the duties incumbent upon him.

2. That of husband and wife, which is founded in nature, but modified by society: the one directing man to
continue and multiply his species, the other prescribing
the manner in which that natural impulse must be confined and regulated.

3. That of parent and child, which is consequential to
that of marriage being its principle and design; and it is
by virtue of this relationship that infants are protected,
maintained and educated.

He further comments on the several sorts of servants:
(1) that of pure slavery, and (2) menial servants; so-
called from being within the walls, or domestics.

The contract between them and their master arises upon the hiring. If the hiring be general without any particular time limited, the law construes it to be a hiring
for one year; upon a principle of natural equity, that the
servant shall serve, and master maintain him, as well
when there is work to be done and when there is not: but
the contract may be made for any longer or shorter term.

There is little difference between the common law and

the present-day law. While today the relationship of master and servant is not capable of exact definition, it may nevertheless be stated broadly that the relationship is that which arises under a contract of employment between a master or employer, on the one hand, and his servant or employee, on the other. The master is deemed to have the superior choice, control and direction of the servant, and whose will the servant represents in the detail as well as the ultimate result of the work.

Servant in its broadest sense includes any person over whom personal authority is exercised, or who asserts himself or labors for the benefit of a master or employer. In more recent times, the words employer and employee have merely supplanted the older term of master and servant. This shift has been due no doubt to the vast increase of employment of skilled persons in industry.

In Biblical times the servant was subject to absolute control of the master, and the servant's labors were solely for the benefit of the master, who had to answer to no one for the treatment accorded the servant, except to God.

"No man can serve two masters" are the words of Matthew, and they are a basic rule of man's guidance.

Escaping servants (slaves) are not to be returned to their master is a provision of Deuteronomy 23 and this was, thousands of years later, rewritten into our various state laws prior to the Civil War.

THE BIBLICAL LAW

No man can serve two masters: for either he will hate the one and love the other; or else he will hold to the one, and despise the other. . . . *Matthew 6:24*

Accuse not a servant unto his master, lest he curse thee, and thou be found guilty. *Proverbs 30:10*

. . . and they drew and lifted up Joseph out of the pit, and sold Joseph to the Ishmeelites for twenty pieces of silver. *Genesis 37:28*

If thy buy a Hebrew servant, six years he shall serve: and in the seventh he shall go out free for nothing.

If he come in by himself, he shall go out by himself; if he were married, then his wife shall go out with him.

If his master have given him a wife, and she have born him sons or daughters; the wife and her children shall be her master's . . . and if the servant shall plainly say I love my master, my wife, and my children; I will not go out free;

Then his master shall bring him unto the judges; . . . and he (the servant) shall serve him forever. *Exodus 21:2, 3, 4, 5, 6*

And if thy brother, an Hebrew man, or an Hebrew woman, be sold unto thee, and serve thee six years; then in the seventh year thou shall let him go free from thee . . . though shalt not let him go away empty: thou shalt furnish him liberally out of thy flock and out of thy floor, and out of thy winepress. . . . *Deuteronomy 15:12, 13*

If a man sell his daughter to be a maidservant, she shall not go out as the menservants do. If she please not her master, who hath betrothed her to himself, then shall he let her be redeemed: to sell her unto a strange nation he shall have no power, seeing he hath dealt deceitfully with her. And if he have betrothed her unto his son, he shall deal with her after the manner of daughters. If he take him another wife; her food, her raiment, and her duty of marriage, shall he not diminish. And if he do not these three unto her, then shall she go out free. . . . *Exodus 21:7, 8, 9, 10, 11*

And ye shall . . . proclaim liberty throughout all the land all the inhabitants thereof . . . and ye shall return every man unto his possession, and ye shall return every man unto his family, (every fiftieth year . . . a jubilee shall the fiftieth year be unto you) *Leviticus 25:10, 11*

That every man should let his manservant, being . . . Hebrew . . . go free . . . (on their return from Babylon). *Jeremiah 34:9*

For they . . . which I brought forth out of the land of Egypt: they shall not be sold as bondsmen. *Leviticus 25:42*

. . . be not yet the servants of men. *1 Corinthians 7:23*

. . . be not entangled again with the yoke of bondage. *Galatians 5:1*

Thou shalt not deliver unto his master the servant which is escaped from his master unto thee; he shall dwell with thee, even among you, in that place which he shall choose in one of thy gates, where it liketh him best: thou shalt not oppress him. *Deuteronomy 23:15, 16*

Send him (Servant) to labor, that he be not idle; for idleness teacheth much evil. *Ecclesiasticus 33:27*

Masters, give unto your servants that which is just and equal. . . . *Colossians 4:1*

Let thy soul love a good servant, and defraud him not of liberty. *Ecclesiasticus 7:21*

And, ye masters forebear . . . threatening . . . *Ephesians 6:9*

And if a man smite his servant, or his maid, with a rod, and he die under his hand: he shall surely be punished. *Exodus 21:20*

And if a man smite the eye of his servant, or the eye of his maid, that it perish; he shall let him go free . . . and if he smite out his manservant's tooth, or his maidservant's tooth; he shall let him go free. . . . *Exodus 21:26, 27*

If thee ox shall push (injure) a manservant, or a maid-servant; (the owner of the ox) shall give unto their master thirty shekels of silver. . . .
Exodus 21:32

A wise servant shall have rule over a son that causeth shame, and shall have part of the inheritance among the brethren.
Proverbs 17:2

Servants be subject to your masters with all fear; not only to the good and gentle, but also to the froward.
1 Peter 2:18

No man can serve two masters: for either he will hate the one, and love the other . . . ye cannot serve God and Mammon.
Matthew 6:24

Masters, give unto your servants that which is just and equal. . . .
Colossians 4:1

. . . Well done, thou good and faithful servant.
Matthew 25:21

. . . There be many servants now a days that break away every man from his master.
1 Samuel 25:10

MILITARY LAW

THERE IS "a time of war, and a time of peace." With this observation Ecclesiastes 3:8 has reviewed the history of warfare through the ages. It is futile to cry "peace, peace, when there is no peace." Thus Jeremiah 6:14 opened the way for the people of Israel to say in I Mac. 2:40 "If we all do as our brethren have done, and fight not for our lives and our laws against the heathen, they will now quickly root us out of the earth."

Whether the prophecy of Isaiah that "the nations shall beat their swords into ploughshares, and their spears into pruning hooks; nation shall not lift up sword against nation, neither shall they learn war any more," will ever be realized by man or not is still a matter of world argument.

There is no Biblical directive against war, in fact in Exodus 15 Moses says "The Lord is a man of war" and in Deuteronomy 20 "who goes with his people, to fight against their enemies."

All men during Biblical days who were from twenty years old and upward, if able to go to war, and not exempt from service had to go forth "armed to battle."

War was a necessity apparently for in Deuteronomy 23 stress is laid upon the need of maintaining sanitary conditions on the field of battle. Definite directions are given for the guidance of troops in the field.

Whether the Mosaic code concerning war was a necessity of the conquest of the Holy Land or whether the laws relative to the military come from primitive sources is of little consequence when it is observed that the laws in this regard today are in fact a re-enactment of those in Exodus, Numbers and Deuteronomy.

THE BIBLICAL LAW

What man is there that has built a new house, and has not dedicated it? let him go and return to his house, lest he die in the battle, and another man dedicate it. And what man is he that hath planted a vineyard, and hath not yet eaten of it? let him also go and return unto his house, lest he die in the battle and another man eat of it. And what man is there that hath betrothed a wife, and hath not taken her? let him go and return unto his house, lest he die in the battle, and another man take her. What man is there that is fearful and faint-hearted? let him go and return unto his house, lest his brethren's heart faint as well as his heart.   *Deuteronomy 20:5, 8*

When a man has taken a new wife, he shall not go out to war . . . but he shall be free at home one year . . .
                    Deuteronomy 24:5

. . . thou shalt save alive nothing that breatheth: but thou shalt utterly destroy them, namely the Hittites, and the Amorites, the Canaanites, and the Perizzites, the Hivites, and the Jebusites . . .   *Deuteronomy 20:16, 17*

There is . . . a time of war, and a time of peace.
                    Ecclesiastes 3:8

When thou goest to war against thine enemies . . . and thou hast taken them captive, and seest among the captives a beautiful woman, and hast a desire unto her, that thou wouldest have her to thy wife: then thou shalt bring her home to thine house . . . and she shall put the raimant of her captivity from off her . . . and bewail her father and her mother a full month: and after that thou shalt go in unto her, and be her husband, and she shall be thy wife. And it shall be, if thou have no delight in her, then thou shall let her go whither she will; but thou shalt not sell her at all for money, thou shalt not make merchandise of her, because thou hast humbled her.   *Deuteronomy 21:10, 14*

When the host goeth forth against thine enemies, then keep thee from every wicked thing. If there be among you any man, that is not clean by reason of uncleanness that

chanceth him by night, then shall he go abroad out of the camp, he shall not come within the camp: But it shall be, when evening cometh on, he shall wash himself with water: and when the sun is down, he shall come into the camp again.
Deuteronomy 23:9, 10, 11

Thou shalt have a place also without the camp, whither thou shalt go forth abroad: and thou shalt have a paddle upon thy weapon; and it shall be, when thou wilt ease thyself abroad out of the camp, he shall not come within the camp: But it shall be, when evening cometh on, he shall wash himself with water: and when the sun is down, he shall come into the camp again.
Deuteronomy 23:9, 10, 11

Thou shalt have a place also without the camp, whither thou shalt go forth abroad: and thou shalt have a paddle upon thy weapon; and it shall be, when thou wilt ease thyself abroad, thou shalt dig therewith, and shalt turn back and cover that which cometh from thee: For the Lord thy God walketh in the midst of thy camp . . . therefore shall thy camp be holy: that he see no unclean thing in thee. . . .
Deuteronomy 23:12, 13, 14

. . . teach them war, at the least such as before knew nothing thereof.
Judges 3:2

What king, going to make war against another king, sitteth not down first, and consulteth whether he be able with ten thousand to meet him that cometh against him with twenty thousand?
Luke 14:31

When Thou comest nigh unto a city to fight against it, then proclaim peace into it. And it shall be, if it make thee answer of peace, and open unto thee, then it shall be, that all the people that is found therein shall be tributaries unto thee.
Deuteronomy 20:10, 11

And if it will make no peace with thee, but will make war against thee, then thou shalt besiege it: and when the Lord thy God hath delivered it into thine hands, thy shalt smite every male thereof with the edge of the sword: . . . thou shalt smite every male thereof with the edge of the sword: but the women, and the little ones, and the cattle, and all that is in the city, even all the spoil thereof, shalt thou take unto thyself.   *Deuteronomy 20:13, 14*

League of Nations

And it came to pass, when all the kings which were on this side Jordan, in the hills, and in the valleys, and in all the coasts of the great sea over against Lebanon, the Hittite, and the Amovite, the Canaanite, the Perizziite, the Hivite, and the Jebusite, heard thereof; that they gathered themselves together, to fight with Joshua and with Israel, with one accord.

Joshua 9:1, 2

OATHS

POSSIBLY THE first oath of record was taken by Abraham from his eldest servant as recorded in Genesis 24: "And Abraham said unto his eldest servant . . . I will make thee swear by the Lord . . . that thou shalt not take a wife unto my son of the daughters of the Canaanites, among whom I dwell: but thou shalt go unto my country, and to my kindred, and take a wife unto my son, Isaac . . . And the servant . . . sware to him concerning the matter."

It is universally understood that by taking an oath, the person so doing imprecates the vengeance of God upon him if the oath he takes is false. This is perhaps based on Deuteronomy 6:13 stating, "Thou shalt fear the Lord Thy God, and serve him, and shalt swear by his name."

An oath is a solemn declaration which is necessary as a condition to the filling of some office more or less public, such as becoming a witness and giving evidence in a court of law. There are assertory oaths, or those by which something is asserted as true, and promissory oaths, of those by which something is promised.

No oath was required under Biblical law. All testimony was received under the admonition of the Ninth Commandment: "Thou shalt not bear false witness against thy neighbor." Philo Judaeus wrote that "whosoever will not tell the truth without an oath, would not scruple to assert falsehood with an oath."

In place of an oath the solemn warning which was administered to each witness in the presence of the entire

171

court admonished him to: "Forget not, O witness, that it is one thing to give evidence in a trial as to money and another in a trial for life. In a money suit, if thy witness-bearing shall do wrong, money may repair that wrong. But in this trial for life, if thou sinnest, the blood of the accused and the blood of his seed to the end of time shall be imputed unto thee. . . . For a man from one signet ring may strike off many impressions, and all of them shall be exactly alike. But He, the King of the kings, He the Holy and the Blessed, has struck off from His type of the first man the forms of all men that shall live, yet so that no one human being is wholly alike to any other. Wherefore let us think and believe that the whole world is created for a man such as he whose life hangs on thy words. But these ideas must not deter thee from testifying to what thou actually knowest. Scripture declares: "The witness who hath seen or known, and doth not tell, shall bear his iniquity." Nor must ye scruple about becoming the instrument of the alleged criminal's death. Remember the Scriptural maxim: 'When the wicked perish, there is shouting.'"

The elements of this preliminary caution were, first, a warning against injustice to the accused; second, a reminder of the retribution of Heaven upon the swearer; third, an admonition against timidity or fear in testifying.

Witnesses gave their testimony separately but always in the presence of the accused. Deuteronomy 19 provides that "the judges shall make diligent inquisition; and, behold, if the witness be a false witness and hath testified falsely against his brother, then shall ye do unto him as he had though to do unto his brother."

THE BIBLICAL LAW

And I will make thee swear by the Lord . . . that thou shalt not take a wife unto my son of the daughters of the Canaanites, among whom I dwell: but thouse shalt go unto my country, and to my kindred and take a wife unto my son Isaac . . . And the servant put his hand under the thigh of Abraham his master, and swore to him concerning that matter.
Genesis 24:2, 3, 4-9

. . . men verily swear by the greater; and an oath for confirmation is to them an end of all strife.   *Hebrews 6:16*

Then shall an oath of the Lord be between them both, that he hath not put his hand unto his neighbor's goods; and the owner of it shall accept thereof . . . *Exodus 22:11*

And the time drew near that Israel must die: and he called his son Joseph, and said unto him . . . put . . . thy hand under my thigh, and deal kindly and truly with me; bury me not . . . in Egypt . . . and he said swear unto me. And he swore unto him.   *Genesis 47:29-31*

Thou shalt fear the Lord thy God, and serve him and shalt swear by his name.   *Deuteronomy 6:13*

Swear not at all; neither by heaven . . . nor by the earth . . .
Matthew 6:34, 35

. . . Swear not, neither by heaven, neither by the earth, neither by any other oath: but let your yea be yea; and your nay, nay. . . .
James 5:12

Lying lips are abomination to the Lord: but they that deal truly are his delight.   *Proverbs 12:22*

. . . he that telleth lies shall not tarry in my sight.
Psalms 101:7

. . . ye shall not swear by my name falsely . . .
Leviticus 19:12

If a man vow a vow . . . or swear an oath to bind his soul with a bond; he shall not break his word, he shall do according to all that proceedeth out of his mouth.
Numbers 30:2

I will perform the oath which I swore. *Genesis 26:3*

OFFENSES AGAINST MORALS

UNDER BIBLICAL LAW the rape of a maiden is not a criminal offense in the strict sense of the word, since it may be expiated by a fine and forced marriage. "If a man find a damsel that is a virgin, that is not betrothed, and he lay hold of her, and lie with her, and they be found; then the man that lay with her shall give unto the damsel's father fifty shekels of silver, and she shall be his wife, because he hath humbled her; he may not put her away all his days."

In the case of seduction, the seducer must pay a dowry for the woman to be his wife: "If her father utterly refuse to give her to him, he shall pay money according to the dowry of virgins." Since the Bible does not specify the amount to be paid by the seducer, it must have been a fixed and accepted amount.

Insolent disregard of moral laws or restraint has been the way of some since the beginning of time. Biblical history cites many instances of sin concerning morals, and it is noteworthy that penalties then as now are generally the same.

The Old Testament unlike the New does not expressly condemn fornication. Many passages of the New Testament denounce this sin. No punishment was prescribed, and there is no evidence of any prosecution for this offense. Under Mosaic law, a virgin that is unbetrothed is guilty of no offense if she has sexual relations with a man; only the enticer is subject to punishment.

Incest is condemned. This sin consists in marriage or

sexual relationship between persons near of kin: "None of you shall approach to any that is near of kin to him, to uncover their nakedness." (Leviticus 18:6)

The punishment for incest was by "cutting off" or death. Leviticus 18:29 provides that whoever shall commit this abomination shall be cut off. It is further provided that death for both participants is the penalty if a man "lieth with his father's wife" and "If a man take a wife and her mother . . . they shall be burnt with fire, both he and they." (Leviticus 20:14)

Sodomy was named after the Sodomites, for which the cities of Sodom and Gomorrah were, according to biblical history, destroyed. Leviticus 18:22 defines the crime as "thou shalt not lie with mankind, as with womankind" and that the penalty is death.

In Romans 1, St. Paul observed that even women changed the natural use into that which is against nature, and that men burned in their lust one toward another.

Rape is committed when a man has sexual relations with a woman not his wife, against her will and without her consent. In Biblical law if committed against a "betrothed damsel" the man is punished with death. If against a virgin, he must marry her, must pay her father fifty shekels of silver, and must mary her. He may never divorce her (Deuteronomy 22:25-29).

Adultery is the voluntary sexual intercourse of a married person with a person other than the offender's husband or wife. Open and notorious adultery is a criminal offense and punished as such.

Let all things be done decently and in order.
1 Corinthians 14:40

. . . in lewdness is decay and great want: for lewdness is the mother of famine. *Tobit 4:13*

Now the works of the flesh are manifest, which are these; adultery, fornication, uncleanness, lasciviousness.
Galatians 5:19

Adultery

Thou shalt not commit adultery. *Exodus 20:14*

. . . I will be a swift witness against . . . the adulterers . . .
Malachi 3:5

So he that goeth into his neighbor's wife; whosoever toucheth her shall not be innocent. *Proverbs 6:29*

But whoso committeth adultery with a woman lacketh understanding: he that doeth it destroyeth his own soul.
Proverbs 6:32

Moreover thou shalt not lie carnally with thy neighbor's wife, to defile thyself with her. *Leviticus 18:20*

Be ashamed . . . to gaze upon another man's wife: or to be overbusy with his maid, and come not near her bed.
Ecclesiasticus 41:17, 21, 22

. . . whosoever looketh on a woman to lust after her hath committed adultery with her already in his heart.
Matthew 5:28

Sit not at all with another man's wife, nor sit down with her in thine arms, and spend not thy money with her at the wine; lest thine heart incline unto her, and so through thy desire thou fall into destruction. *Ecclesiasticus 9:9*

[He that hath] defiled his neighbor's wife . . . shall surely die.   *Ezekiel 18:11, 13*

And the man that committeth adultery with another man's wife, even he that committeth adultery with his neighbor's wife, the adulterer and the adulteress shall surely be put to death.   *Leviticus 20:10*

If a man be found lying with a woman married to an husband, then they shall both of them die, both the man that lay with the woman, and the woman.   *Deuteronomy 22:22*

And whosoever lieth carnally with a woman, that is a bonds-maid, betrothed to an husband, and not at all redeemed, nor freedom given her; she shall be scourged; they shall not be put to death, because she was not free.   *Leviticus 19:20*

If a damsel that is a virgin be betrothed unto a husband; and a man find her in the city, and lie with her; then ye shall . . . stone them with stones that they die; the damsel, because she cried not, being in the city; and the man, because he hath humbled his neighbour's wife. . . .   *Deuteronomy 22: 23, 24*

Bestiality

Neither shalt thou lie with any beast to defile thyself therewith: neither shall any woman stand before a beast to lie down thereto . . .   *Leviticus 18:23*

And if a man lie with a beast, he shall surely be put to death: and ye shall slay the beast.   *Leviticus 20:15*

And if a woman approach unto any beast, and lie down thereto, thou shalt kill the woman, and the beast. . . .
                                        Leviticus 20:16

Whosoever lieth with a beast shall surely be put to death.
                                        Exodus 22:19

Fornication

Flee fornication. Every sin that a man doeth is without the body; but he that committeth fornication sinneth against his own body.   *1 Corinthians 6:18*

Neither let us commit fornication. . . .   *1 Corinthians 10:8*

Incest

None of you shall approach to any that is near of kin to him, to uncover their nakedness. . . .   *Leviticus 18:6*

For whosoever shall commit any . . . abomination [incest]. . . . shall be cut off from among their people. *Leviticus 18:29*

Menstruous Women

And if a woman have an issue, and her issue in her flesh be blood, she shall be put apart seven days: and whosoever toucheth her shall be unclean.   *Leviticus 15:19*

And if a man shall lie with a woman having her sickness . . . both of them shall be cut off from their people.
                                             Leviticus 20:18

Rape

And if a man entice a maid that is not betrothed, and lie with her, he shall surely endow her to be his wife.
If her father utterly refuse to give her unto him, he shall pay money according to the dowry of virgins.
                                            Exodus 22:16, 17

If a damsel that is a virgin be betrothed unto an husband and a man find her in the city and lie with her . . . ye shall stone them . . . that they die; the damsel, because she cried not, being in the city; and the man, because he hath humbled his neighbor's wife . . .   *Deuteronomy 22: 23, 24*

But if a man find a betrothed damsel in the field, and the man force her, and lie with her: then the man only . . . shall die.   *Deuteronomy 22:25*

If a man find a damsel that is a virgin, which is not betrothed, and lay hold on her, and lie with her . . . then the man . . . shall give unto the damsel's father fifty shekels of silver, and she shall be his wife . . . he may not put her away all his days.   *Deuteronomy 22:28, 29*

Sodomy

Thou shallt not lie with mankind, as with womankind: it is an abomination.   *Leviticus 18:22*

If a man also lie with mankind, as he lieth with a woman, both of them have committed an abomination: they shall surely be put to death.   · *Leviticus 20:13*

PARENT AND CHILD

UNDER THE common law, children were of two sorts—legitimate and spurious, or bastards. A legitimate child is he that is born in lawful wedlock, or within a competent time afterwards. In this relationship the duty of parents to provide for the maintenance of their children is a principle of natural law; an obligation laid on them not only by natural duties, but by their own act, in bringing them into the world; for they would be in the highest manner injurious to their issue, if they only gave their children life, that they might afterwards see them perish. By begetting them, therefore, they have entered into a voluntary obligation, to endeavor as far as in them lies, that the life which they have bestowed shall be supported and preserved. Thus, the child has a perfect right of receiving maintenance from their parents.

Marriage in all civilized states is built on the natural obligation of the father to provide for his child; for that ascertains and makes known the person who is bound to fulfill this obligation; whereas, in promiscuous and illicit conjunctions, the father is unknown, and the mother finds a thousand obstacles in her way—shame, remorse, the restrictions of her sex, and the rigor of laws that stifle her inclinations to perform this duty; and besides, she generally lacks ability.

The laws of all well regulated states have taken care to enforce the duty of parental support, though providence has done it more effectually than any law, by implanting in the breast of every parent that natural, or insuperable degree of affection, which not even the deformity of person or mind, not even the wickedness, ingratitude, or the rebellion of child, can totally suppress or extinguish.

It is common knowledge that those who are taught to respect parental authority in their early years also conform to the laws of the land and the conventions of society throughout their adult life.

Much consideration is given this subject in the Mosaic law, and one of the ten commandments is: "Thou shalt honor thy father and thy mother."

THE BIBLICAL LAW

Honor thy father and mother. . . .   *Exodus 20:12*

A bastard shall not enter into the congregation of the Lord; even to his tenth generation shall he not enter into the congregation of the Lord.   *Deuteronomy 23:2*

For better it is that thy children should seek to thee, than that thou shouldest stand to their courtesy.
     Ecclesiasticus 33:21

Desire not a multitude of unprofitable children, neither delight in ungodly sons . . . and better it is to die without children, than to have them that are ungodly.
     Ecclesiasticus 16:1, 3

He that begetteth a fool doeth it to his sorrow.
     Proverbs 17:21

Thus shall it go also with the wife that leaveth her husband, and bringeth an heir by another . . . her children shall not take root, and her branches shall bring forth no fruit.
     Ecclesiasticus 23:22, 25

And this one woman said, O my lord, I and this woman dwell in one house; and I was delivered of a child with her in the house.

And it came to pass the third day after that I was delivered, that this woman was delivered also; and we were together; there was no stranger with us in the house . . .

And this woman's child died in the night because she overlaid it. And she arose at midnight, and took my son from beside me, while thine handmaid slept, and laid it in her bosom, and laid her dead child in my bosom.

And when I rose in the morning to give my child suck, behold it was dead: but when I had considered it in the morning, behold, it was not my son, which I did bear.

And the other woman said, Nay . . . and the King said, bring me a sword, and they brought a sword before the King.

And the King said, divide the living child in two, and give half to one and half to the other. Then spake the woman whose the living child was unto the King, for her bowels yearned upon her son, and she said, O my Lord, give her the living child, and in no wise slay it. But the other said, Let it be neither mine nor thine, but divide it.

Then the King answered and said, Give her the living child, and in no wise slay it: she is the mother thereof.

1 Kings 3:16, 27

For the Lord hath given the father honor over the children, and hath confirmed the authority of the mother over the sons.

Ecclesiasticus 3:2

Chasten thy son while there is hope, and let not thy soul spare for his crying. *Proverbs 22:15*

Correct thy son, and he shall give thee rest; yea, he shall give delight unto thy soul. *Proverbs 29:17*

The rod and reproof give wisdom: but a child left to himself bringeth his mother to shame. *Proverbs 29:15*

. . . take wives for your sons, and give your daughters to husbands . . . that ye may be increased . . . *Jeremiah 29:6*

Hast thou daughters? . . . Marry thy daughter . . but give her to a man of understanding. *Ecclesiasticus 7:24, 25*

Ye shall fear every man his mother, and his father. . . .

Leviticus 19:3

He that feareth the Lord will honor his father, and will do service unto his parents . . . *Ecclesiasticus 3:7*

My son, keep thy father's commandment, and forsake not the law of thy mother. *Proverbs 6:20*

And he that curseth his father, or his mother, shall surely be put to death. *Exodus 21:17*

Whoso robbeth his father or his mother, and saith, it is no transgression; the same is the companion of a destroyer.
Proverbs 28:24

. . . ye shall command your children to observe to do, all the words of this law. *Deuteronomy 32:46*

Train up a child in the way he should go: and when he is old, he will not depart from it. *Proverbs 22:6*

Fathers, provoke not your children to anger, lest they be discouraged. *Colossians 3:21*

. . . Thy servant my husband is dead . . . and the creditor is come to take unto him my two sons to be bondsmen.
Kings 4:1

But forasmuch as he had not to pay, his lord commanded him to be sold, and his wife, and children, and all that he had, and payment to be made. *Matthew 18:25*

He that loveth his son causeth him oft to feel the rod, that he may have joy in him in the end. *Ecclesiasticus 30:1*

He that maketh too much of his son shall bind up his wounds . . . an horse not broken becometh headstrong: as a child left to himself will be willful. *Ecclesiasticus 30:7, 8*

Give him no liberty in his youth, and wink not at his follies.
Ecclesiasticus 30:11

Chastise thy son, and hold him to labor, lest his lewd behavior be an offense unto thee. *Ecclesiasticus 7:24*

Keep a sure watch over a shameless daughter . . .
Ecclesiasticus 42:11

. . . for the children ought not lay up (financial provision) for the parents, but the parents for the children.

2 Corinthians 12:14

Remember thy father and thy mother, when thy sittest among great men. Be not forgetful before (of) them.

Ecclesiasticus 23:14

Remember that thou wast begotten of them; and how canst thou recompense them the things that they have done for thee?

Ecclesiasticus 7:28

Help thy father in his age, and grieve him not as long as he liveth. And if his understanding fail, have patience with him . . .

Ecclesiasticus 3:12, 13

He that forsaketh his father is as a blasphemer . . .

Ecclesiasticus 3:16

. . . the heir, as long as he is a child, differeth nothing from a servant, though he be lord of all.

Galatians 4:1

Unto the woman [God] said, I will greatly multiply thy sorrow and thy conception; in sorrow thou wilt bring forth children. . . .

Genesis 3:16

Chasten thy son while there is hope, and let not thy soul spare for his crying.

Proverbs 19:18

. . . do not sin against the child . . .

Genesis 42:22

If thy daughter be shameless, keep her in straitly, lest she abuse herself through overmuch liberty. *Ecclesiasticus 26:10*

Hast thou children? instruct them, and bow down their neck from their youth.

Ecclesiasticus 7:23

Withhold not correction from the child: for if thou beatest him with the rod, he shall not die.

Proverbs 23:13

An horse not broken becometh headstrong: and a child left to himself will be wilful. *Ecclesiasticus 30:8*

Children, obey your parents in all things: for this is well pleasing to the Lord. *Colossians 3:20*

PARTNERSHIP

GENERALLY, a partnership is an association of two or more persons for carrying on some business or undertaking. All history has recorded partnership arrangements and the Bible, not only refers to them, but advises the course of conduct to be followed by partners.

Wherever and whenever man creates an association of two or more people who contribute money or property to carry on a joint business and who share profits or losses in certain proportion, there will always be the necessity for rules of conduct.

In our laws today, partnership is one of mutual trust and fair dealing. The statutes are so many that thought must be given to the many weaknesses in this type of business arrangement. In Biblical times, as today, man is well advised to "be not ashamed of reckoning with thy partners."

THE BIBLICAL LAW

Be ashamed . . . of unjust dealing before thy partner. . . .
Ecclesiasticus 41:17, 18

Be not ashamed . . . of reckoning with thy partners.
Ecclesiasticus 42:1, 3

Whoso is partner with a thief hateth his own soul.
Proverbs 29:24

And so was also James and John, the sons of Zebedee, which were partners with Simon . . . *Luke 5:10*

Whether any do inquire of Titus, he is my partner and fellow-helper. . . . *11 Corinthians 8:23*

If thou count me therefore a partner, receive him as myself. If he hath wronged thee, or oweth thee aught, put that on mine account. *Philemon 17, 18*

PENALTIES

OFFENSES COMMITTED against the person—murder, mayhem, assault, incest, and adultery, are considered not only sins against the Divinity but also crimes against organized society. These offenses brought either capital punishment or punishment by the lex talionis. By the lex talionis, the court inflicts upon the culprit the very injury which he has inflicted upon his victim: "Eye for eye, tooth for tooth, hand for hand, foot for foot, burning for burning, wound for wound, stripe for stripe."

The Scripture reads: "And if a man maim his neighbor, as he hath done, so shall it be done to him: breach for breach, eye for eye, tooth for tooth; as he hath maimed a man, so shall it be rendered unto him."

The lex talionis may seem barbarous and inhuman, but the principle of "life for life, eye for eye" established a fixed limit to retaliatory punishment. It substituted for the savage, primitive concept of limitless revenge and private resentment, a legal punishment as commensurate as possible with the injury inflicted. St. Augustine wrote that the lex talionis was a law of justice, not of hatred; one eye, not two eyes, for an eye; one tooth, not ten teeth, for a tooth; one life, not a whole family, for a life.

The Jews, however, from the earliest times, were dissatisfied with the literal interpretation of this Biblical directive. They held that the rule "eye for eye" had reference to the more humane law of compensation in money. Mayhem was thus made a fineable offense.

There was another offense, that of the false witness, which was considered a crime against the commonwealth and subject to the lex talionis. Of the false witness, the bible prescribes: "Then shall you do unto him as he purposed to do unto his neighbor . . . and ye shall have no pity: life for life, eye for eye, tooth for tooth, hand for hand, foot for foot."

In the Bible there is no mention of prisons—the closest was a ward which is described as a place of detention, where the law-breaker was held until he was brought to justice.

Cities of Refuge were established for the unintentional murderer. The primary object of these cities of refuge was to protect the unintentional murderer from the family avenger, who might otherwise slay him without due process of law. In Numbers we read: "Ye shall appoint you cities of refuge for you, that the manslayer that killeth any person through error may flee thither. And the cities shall be unto you for refuge from the avenger, that the manslayer die not, until he stand before the congregation for judgment." It would seem from such wording that the cities of refuge were non-penal in character.

However, Numbers also provides that the cities of refuge shall serve not only as a sanctuary for the manslayer, but also as a place of detention until the death of the high priest, and the text reads: "Then the congregation shall judge between the smiter and the avenger of blood according to these ordinances, and the congregation restore him to the city of refuge, whither he was fled; and he shall dwell therein until the death of the high priest, who was anointed with the holy oil."

Manslaughter was the only Biblical crime punishable by imprisonment and then only within a city of refuge. The character of the city of refuge, however, was an ordinary city and the manslayer was safe so long as he remained within its limits.

The latter Numbers text recognizes the right of the family avenger to kill the manslayer upon sight, if found outside the city during his period of confinement. The Biblical text reads: "But if the manslayer shall at any time go beyond the border of his city of refuge, and the avenger of blood slay the manslayer; there shall be no blood-guiltiness for him; because he must remain in his city of refuge until the death of the high priest; but after the death of the high priest, the manslayer may return into the land of his possession."

In Deuteronomy, the unintentional manslayer is likewise mentioned twice. Both texts re-state that the purpose of the cities of refuge is to protect the manslayer. The first reference reads: "That the manslayer might flee thither, that slayeth his neighbor unawares, and hated him not in time past; and that fleeing into one of these cities he may live."

The second Deuternomic text directs: "And this is the case of the manslayer, that shall flee thither and live. . . . He shall flee unto one of these cities and live; lest the avenger of blood pursue the manslayer, while his heart is hot, whereas he was not deserving of death, inasmuch as he hated him not in time past. Therefore I command thee saying: "Thou shalt separate three cities for thee."

There is an additional command that the roads leading to the cities of refuge be kept in perfect condition and be clearly designated, so that the manslayer may experience no difficulty in getting there. The second Deuteronomic text directs that "Thou shalt prepare thee the way, and divide the borders of the land, which the Lord thy God causeth thee to inherit, into three parts, that every manslayer may flee thither."

The procedure by which a manslayer is admitted into one of the cities of refuge is described in Joshua: "And the Lord spoke unto Joshua, saying 'Speak unto the children of Israel, saying: Assign you three cities of refuge, whereof I spoke unto you by the hand of Moses; that the manslayer that killeth any person through error and unawares may flee thither; and they shall be unto you for a refuge from the avenger of blood. And he shall flee unto one of those cities, and shall stand at the entrance of the gate of the city, and declare his cause in the ears of the elders of the city; and they shall take him into the city unto them, and give him a place, that he may dwell among them. And if the avenger of blood pursue after him, then shall they not deliver up the manslayer into his hand, because he smote his neighbor unawares, and hated him not before time. And he shall dwell in that city, until he stand before the congregation for judgment, until the death of the high priest that shall be in those days; then may the manslayer return, and come into his own city, and unto his own house, unto the city from whence he fled."

It appears therefore that the manslayer could not enter a city of refuge at will. Before being admitted, the manslayer must first state his case to a tribunal consisting of the elders of the city who first decide whether or not the case is one of manslaughter, and consequently whether it is one over which the city authorities have jurisdiction. If this tribunal finds him guilty of manslaughter, he may remain in the city of refuge.

THE BIBLICAL LAW

Mercy is seasonable in the time of affliction, as clouds of rain in the time of draught.   *Ecclesiasticus 35:20*

Be not deceived . . . for whatsoever a man swoeth, that shall he also reap.   *Galatians 6:7*

A good man obtaineth favor of the Lord: but a man of wicked devices will he condemn.   *Proverbs 12:2*

For the upright shall dwell in the land, and the perfect shall remain in it. But the wicked shall be cut off from the earth, and the transgressors shall be rooted out of it.   *Proverbs 2:21, 22*

I will destroy all the wicked of the land.   *Psalms 101:8*

And the man that will do presumptuously, and will not hearken unto thee . . . judge, even that man shall die. . . .
                                                    Deuteronomy 17:12

He that despised Moses' law died without mercy under two or three witnesses.   *Hebrews 10:28*

For whosoever shall keep the whole law, and yet offend in one point, he is guilty of all.   *James 2:10*

And whosoever shall trangress the law . . . shall be punished diligently, whether it be by death, or other punishment, by penalty of money, or by imprisonment.   *1 Esdras 8:24*

For everyone that curseth his father or his mother shall be surely put to death.   *Leviticus 20:9*

He that leadeth unto captivity shall go into captivity: he that killeth with the sword must be killed with the sword.
                                                    Revelation 13:10

I, the Lord search the heart . . . even to give every man according to his ways, and according to the fruit of his doings.
                                                    Jeremiah 17:10

And if a man cause a blemish in his neighbor; as he hath done, so shall it be done to him. Breach for breach, eye for eye, tooth for tooth.   *Leviticus 24:19, 20*

Whoso sheddeth man's blood, by man shall his blood be shed . . .   *Genesis 9:6*

And whosoever will not do the law of thy God, and the law of the king, let judgment be executed speedily upon him, whether it be unto death, or to banishment, or to confiscation of goods, or to imprisonment.   *Ezra 7:26*

. . . they caught Paul & Silas . . . and brought them to the magistrates saying, These men being Jews, do exceedingly trouble our city, and teach customs, which are not lawful for us to receive . . . being Romans . . . and the magistrates rent off their clothes, and commanded to beat them . . . and they cast them into prison.   *Acts 16:19, 20, 21, 22, 23*

. . . if the wicked man be worthy to be beaten, that the judge shall cause him to lie down, and to be beaten before his face, according to his fault . . . forty stripes he may give him, and not exceed. . . .   *Deuteronomy 25:2, 3*

When the righteous turneth from his righteousness, and committeth iniquity, he shall even die thereby.   *Ezekiel 33:18*

. . . the righteousness of the righteous shall not deliver him in the day of his transgression . . . neither shall the righteous be able to live for his righteousness in the day that he sinneth.   *Ezekiel 33:12*

. . . if he [the righteous] trust to his own righteousness, and commit iniquity, all his righteousness shall not be remembered; but for his iniquity that he hath committed, he shall die for it.   *Ezekiel 33:13*

And thine eye shall not pity; but life shall go for life, eye for eye, tooth for tooth, hand for hand, foot for foot.   *Deuteronomy 19:21*

He [God] hath mercy on them . . . that diligently seek after his judgments.   *Ecclesiasticus 18:14*

The Lord is slow to anger . . . and will not at all acquit the wicked . . .   *Nahum 1:13*

For the Lord will not be slack . . . till he hath smitten in sunder the loins of the unmerciful and . . . till he have taken away the multitude of the proud, and broken the sceptre of the unrighteous.   *Ecclesiasticus 35:18*

Till he [God] have rendered to every man according to his deeds, and to the works of men according to their devices; till he have judged the cause of his people, and made them to rejoice in his mercy.   *Ecclesiasticus 35:19*

For he shall have judgment without mercy, that hath showed no mercy . . .   *James 2:13*

If the wicked . . . give again that he had robbed, walk in the statutes of life, without committing iniquity . . he shall not die.   *Ezekiel 33:15*

He that saith unto the wicked, thou art righteous; him shall the people curse . . .   *Proverbs 24:24*

He that justifieth the wicked, and he that condemneth the just, even they both are abomination to the Lord.
                                      Proverbs 17:15

They that forsake the law praise the wicked: but such as keep the law contend with them.   *Proverbs 28:4*

Let favor be shewed to the wicked, yet will he not learn righteousness: in the land of uprightness will he deal unjustly. . . .   *Isaiah 26:10*

Who knowing the judgment of God, that they which commit such things are worthy of death, not only do the same, but have pleasure in them that do them.   *Romans 1:32*

Woe unto them that call evil good, and good evil; that put darkness for light, and light for darkness; that put bitter for sweet and sweet for bitter. *Isaiah 5:20*

Moreover ye shall take no satisfaction for the life of a murderer, which is guilty of death: but he shall surely be put to death. And ye shall take no satisfaction for him that is fled to the city of his refuge. . . .

And if a man take a wife and her mother . . . they shall be burnt with fire, both he and they . . . *Leviticus 20:14*

And the daughter of any priest, if she profane herself by playing the whore . . . she shall be burnt with fire . . .

Leviticus 21:9

Cities of Refuge

. . . if the [the slayer] thrust him suddenly without enmity, or have cast upon him anything without laying of wait, or with

a stone . . . seeing him not, and cast it upon him, that he die, and was not his enemy, neither sought his harm. . . .

Numbers 35:22, 23

. . . . there shall be . . . cities for refuge, which ye shall appoint . . . that the slayer may flee thither, which killeth any person at unawares.

And they shall be . . . cities for refuge from the avenger; that the manslayer die not, until he stand before the congregation in judgment. *Numbers 35:6, 11, 12*

Then Moses severed three cities . . . that the slayer might flee thither, which should kill his neighbor unawares, and hated him not in times past; and that fleeing into one of these cities he might live. *Deuteronomy 4:41, 42*

Excusable Homicide

And this is the case of the slayer, which shall flee thither [City of refuge] that he may live; whoso killeth his neighbor ignorantly, whom he hated not in time past; as when goeth

into the wood with his neighbor to hew wood, and his hand
fetcheth a stroke with the axe to cut down the tree, and the
head slippeth from the helve, and lighteth upon his neighbor,
that he die; he shall flee unto one of those cities, and live: lest
the avenger of the blood pursue the slayer, while his heart is
hot, and overtake him . . . and slay him; whereas he was not
worthy of death, inasmuch as he hated him not in time past.

Deuteronomy 19:4, 5, 6

And if the avenger of blood pursue after him, then they
shall not deliver the slayer up into his hand; because he
smote his neighbor unwittingly, and hated him not beforetime.

Joshua 20:5

Kidnaping

And he that stealeth a man, and selleth him . . . he shall
surely be put to death.   *Exodus 21:16*

If a man be found stealing any of his brethren of the children
of Israel, and maketh merchandize of him, or selleth him; then
that thief shall die. . . .   *Deuteronomy 24:7*

Probation

But if the wicked will turn from all his sins that he hath
committed . . . and do that which is lawful and right, he shall
surely live, he shall not die. All his transgressions . . . they
shall not be mentioned him. . . .   *Ezekiel 18:21*

And [they] brought unto him a woman taken in adultery . . .
they say unto him . . . Moses in the law commanded us,
that such should be stoned: but what sayest thou? . . . but
Jesus . . . said unto them, he that is without sin among you,
let him first cast a stone at her . . . and Jesus said unto her
. . . go and sin no more.   *John 8:3, 11*

Reproach not a man that turneth from sin [crime], but
remember that we are all worthy of punishment.

Ecclesiasticus 8:5

If we have no sin, we deceive ourselves, and the truth is not
in us.   *1 John 1:8*

PERJURY

PERJURY IS THE giving of false testimony under oath before any competent tribunal, officer or person by making a false statement, or by making a false affidavit before any person authorized to administer oaths. Any person who willfully and contrary to his oath states as true any material matter which he knows to be false has committed perjury.

In the law today the terms false swearing and perjury are used interchangeably. Perjury involves the making of a false statement oral or written. The statement must be as to a material pertinent fact. This type of statement is to be differentiated from a statement of opinion or belief, except that if a person willfully swears to a belief of fact which he knows does not exist, he is guilty of perjury.

In Biblical law the rule was that "thou shalt near bear false witness against thy neighbor." This one law if followed completely would obviate the necessity of legal and technical definitions of the offense of perjury. Whether man can morally and intellectually live within this Mosaic directive is a subject of philosophical conjecture, but Ecclesiasticus agrees that "the law shall be found perfect without lies" and that "a thief is better than a man that is accustomed to lie."

THE BIBLICAL LAW

Thou shalt not bear false witness against thy neighbor.
Exodus 20:16

And let none of you imagine evil in your hearts against his neighbor; and love no false oath . . .   *Zechariah 8:17*

These . . . things doth the Lord hate: a false witness that speaketh lies, and he that soweth discord . . . *Proverbs 6:16, 19*

A false witness shall perish. . . .   *Proverbs 21:28*

Be not a witness against thy neighbor without cause; and deceive not with thy lips.   *Proverbs 24:28*

And ye shall not swear by my name falsely. . . .
Leviticus 19:12

Neither shalt thou bear false witness against thy neighbor.
Deuteronomy 5:20

. . . put not thine hand with the wicked to be an unrighteous witness.   *Exodus 23:1*

The law shall be found perfect without lies: and wisdom is perfection to a faithful mouth.   *Ecclesiasticus 34:8*

A false witness shall not be unpunished, and he that speaketh lies shall not escape.   *Proverbs 18:5*

. . . if the witness be a false witness, and hath testified falsely against his brother; then shall ye do unto him, as he had thought to have done unto his brother. . . .   *Deuteronomy 19:18, 19*

. . . he that telleth lies shall not tarry in my sight.
Psalms 101:7

Keep thee far from a false matter.   *Exodus 23:7*

A thief is better than a man that is accustomed to lie.
Ecclesiasticus 20:25

PHYSICIANS AND MEDICINE

A PHYSICIAN is one who practices the art of healing, preserving and promoting health, and is one who prescribes remedies for the diseases of mankind. In the legal sense, he is, of course, required to be licensed to practice medicine.

Each state has certain requirements which must be met by one seeking to practice medicine. This was not the rule in Biblical days when medical knowledge was limited and it was not necessary for man to become specifically educated in the use of this science. Nor does the Bible provide for the physician and patient relationship, so that whatever is said between them is privileged and confidential and the patient's secrets in the keeping of his physician become inviolable.

There did exist in Biblical days the office of physician. According to many writings, Luke was a physician. The Bible is also inattentive to medicine itself, but refers in several places to the use of a physic. It does point out that God created medicines out of the earth and that such medicines should be used. Of course, we know today that many of the saving medicines which have been used to benefit mankind are produced from the earth. We must assume that the writers of the Bible had some understanding of the healing qualities of the earth on which we live.

It is interesting to speculate on the mention in the Bible of the first anaesthetic administered—"the Lord God caused a deep sleep to fall upon Adam, and he slept;

and he took one of his ribs and closed up the flesh instead thereof."

As early as Genesis 50:2 "Joseph commanded his servants, the physicians, to embalm his father."

Apothecaries, or druggists were known in biblical times. They compounded the incense and holy anointing oils used in religious ceremonies; also, flavoring extracts and medicinal herbs (Exodus 30:25). They were also the undertakers and prepared spices used in burials (2 Chronicles 16:14).

. . . use physic . . . even thou be sick. *Ecclesiasticus 18:19*

The Lord hath created medicines out of the earth; and he that is wise will not abhor them. *Ecclesiasticus 38:4*

And by the river upon the bank thereof . . . shall grow all trees . . . and the fruit thereof shall be for meat, and the leaf thereof for medicine. *Ezekiel 47:12*

Let them take a lump of figs, and lay it for a plaster upon the boil, and he shall recover. *Isaiah 38:21*

. . . in thy sickness be not negligent . . . then give place to the physician, for the Lord hath created him: let him not go from thee . . . there is a time when in their hands there is good success. *Ecclesiasticus 38:9, 12, 13*

A merry heart doth good like a medicine: but a broken spirit drieth the bones. *Proverbs 17:22*

. . . in his disease he sought not the Lord, but to the physicians. *2 Chronicles 16:12*

. . . ye are all physicians of no value. *Job 13:4*

Is there no balm in Gilead; is there no physician there? *Jeremiah 8:22*

The physician cutteth off a long disease; and he that is today a king tomorrow shall die. *Ecclesiasticus 10:10*

Honor a physician with the honor due unto him for the uses which ye may have of him. . . . *Ecclesiasticus 38:1*

. . . They that be whole need not a physician, but they that are sick. *Matthew 9:12*

Ye will surely say unto me this proverb, physician, heal thyself. . . . *Luke 4:23*

Apothecaries

Of such doth the apothecary make a confection; and of his works there is no end. . . . *Ecclesiasticus 37:8*

PROPERTY

UNDER BIBLICAL law the whole earth and all property belongs to God. The 49th Psalm philosophically evaluates man's ownership of property and possessions: ". . . wise men die, likewise the fool and the brutish person perish, and leave their wealth to others. Their inward thought is, that their houses shall continue forever, and their dwelling places to all generations: they call their lands after their own names. Nevertheless man . . . abideth not: he is like the beasts that perish . . . for when he dieth he shall carry nothing away."

As Sir William Blackstone in his Commentaries on the law wrote: "the earth and all things therein were the general property of mankind for the immediate gift of the Creator. . . . Thus the ground was in common, and no part was the permanent property of any man in particular; yet whoever was in the occupation of any determined spot of it, for rest, for shade, or the like, acquired for the time a sort of ownership, from which it would have been unjust and contrary to the law of nature to have driven him by force, but the instant that he quitted the use or occupation of it, another might seize it without injustice."

Property formerly owned, then sold may be redeemed under Biblical law. Redemption laws are not new to our jurisprudence, and are to be found applying in matters pertaining to mortgage foreclosures, particularly of homes when such foreclosures are made by the state. Mosaic law provides for redemption so that the tribal properties may remain intact.

THE BIBLICAL LAW

... I am God ... every beast of the forest is mine, and the cattle upon a thousand hills ... the wild beasts of the field are mine ... the world is mine, and the fulness thereof.

Psalms 50:7, 10, 11, 12

... one born in my house is mine heir. *Genesis 15:3*

A good man leaveth an inheritance to his children's children ...

Proverbs 13:22

... but he that shall come forth out of thine own bowels shall be thine heir. *Genesis 15:4*

If a man hath two wives, one beloved, and another hated ... and if the first born son be hers that was hated: then ... when he maketh his sons inherit that which he hath ... he shall acknowledge the son of the hated for firstborn, by giving him a double portion of all that he hath.

Deuteronomy 21:15, 16, 17

And Esau said to Jacob, feed me ... for I am faint: and Jacob said, sell me this day thy birthright ... and he sold his birthright unto Jacob. *Genesis 25:30, 31, 32, 33*

... men ... leave the rest of their substance to their babes.

Psalms 17:14

And Abraham gave all that he had unto Isaac. But unto the sons of the concubines, Abraham gave gifts ...

Genesis 25:5, 6

Thou shalt not inherit in our father's house; for thou art the son of a strange woman. *Judges 11:2*

... if a man die, and have no son, then ye shall cause his inheritance to pass unto his daughter. And if he have no daughter, then ye shall give his inheritance unto his brethren. And if he have no brethren, then ye shall give his inheritance unto his father's brethren. And if his father have no brethren, then ye shall give his inheritance unto his kinsman that is next to him of his family, and he shall possess it.

Numbers 27:8, 9, 10, 11

. . . if the prince give a gift unto any of his sons, the inheritance thereof shall be his sons' . . . but if he give a gift of his inheritance to one of his servants, then it shall be his to the year of liberty; after it shall return to the prince; but his inheritance shall be his sons' for them. *Ezekiel 46:16, 17*

. . . let them marry to whom they think best; only to the family of the tribe of their father shall they marry. So shall not the inheritance of the children of Israel remove from tribe to tribe: for every one of the children of Israel shall keep himself to the inheritance of the tribe of his fathers. And every daughter, that possesseth an inheritance in any tribe of the children of Israel, shall be wife unto one of the family of the tribe of her father, that the children of Israel may enjoy every man the inheritance of his fathers. Neither shall the inheritance remove from one tribe to another tribe; but everyone of the tribes of the children of Israel shall keep himself to his own inheritance.
Numbers 36:6, 7, 8, 9

The land shall not be sold forever: for the land is mine . . .
Leviticus 25:23

Redemption of Sold Property

And in all the land of your possession ye shall grant a redemption for the land.

If thy brother be waxen poor, and hath sold away some of his possession, and if any of his kin come to redeem it, then shall he redeem that which his brother sold.

And if the man have none to redeem it, and himself be able to redeem it;

Then let him count the years of the sale thereof, and restore the overplus unto the man to whom he sold it; that he may return unto his possession. *Leviticus 25:24, 25, 26, 27, 28*

And if a man sell a dwellinghouse in a walled city, then he may redeem it within a whole year after it is sold. . . .

And if it be not redeemed within the space of a full year, then the house that is in the walled city shall be established for ever to him that bought it throughout his generations.

But the houses of the villages which have no wall round about them shall be counted as the fields of the country: they may be redeemed. . . . *Leviticus 25:29, 30, 31*

PROSTITUTION

PROSTITUTION is defined as promiscuous unchastity for gain. It was not an offense under the common law of England, nor is it synonymous with concubinage and other terms indicating a more restricted degree of abandonment. As ordinarily used in its application to lewd women, it does not refer to sexual intercourse with but one man. However illicit the relation may be, so long as the woman remains faithful to one lover, and is motivated only by affection or passion and not pecuniary gain, she is not, in the language of the law, termed a prostitute.

Prostitution is coeval with society. It stains the earliest mythological records. It is constantly assumed as an existing fact in biblical history, and rules of law were promulgated to curb this sin. There was no prohibition against possessing concubines in such number as man desired.

As early as the Bible of Genesis (38:16, 17) Tamar said to Judah: "what wilt thou give me, that thou mayest come in unto me? and he said, I will send thee a kid from the flock. And she said, wilt thou give me a pledge, till thou send it?"

Prostitution was recognized as an existing sin, biblical law providing that "there shall be no whore of the daughters of Israel."

THE BIBLICAL LAW

Whoredom and wine . . . take away the heart. *Hosea 4:11*

Beware of all whoredom. . . .   *Tobit 4:12*

. . . the law is not made for a righteous man, but for the lawless . . . for whoremongers [and] for them that defile themselves with mankind . . .   *1 Timothy 9, 10*

. . . no whoremonger . . . hath any inheritance in the kingdom of . . . God.   *Ephesians 5:5*

Marriage is honorable in all, and the bed undefiled: but whoremongers . . . God will judge.   *Hebrews 13:4*

What wilt thou give me, that thou mayest come in unto me? and he said, I will send thee a kid from the flock. And she said, wilt thou give me a pledge, till thou send it?
                    Genesis 38:16, 17, 18

But the . . . whoremongers . . . shall have their part in the lake which burneth with fire and brimstone . . .
                    Revelation 21:8

Do not prostitute thy daughter, to cause her to be a whore . . .
                    Leviticus 19:29

There shall be no whore of the daughters of Israel. . . .
                    Deuteronomy 23:17

. . . thou shalt not play the harlot . . .   *Hosea 3:3*

She also lieth in wait as for a prey, and increaseth the transgressors among men.   *Proverbs 23:28*

And the daughter of any priest, if she profane herself by playing the whore . . . she shall be burnt with fire.
                    Leviticus 21:9

An harlot shall be accounted as spittle . . .
                    Ecclesiasticus 26:22

Give not thy soul unto harlots, that thou lose not thine
inheritance. *Ecclesiasticus 9:6*

Meet not with an harlot, lest thou fall into her snares.
Ecclesiasticus 9:3

Be ashamed of whoredom . . . *Ecclesiasticus 41:17*

Wine and women will make men of understanding to fall
away: and he that cleaveth to harlots will become impudent.
Moths and worms shall have him to heritage.
Ecclesiasticus 19:2, 3

For by means of a whorish woman a man is brought to a
piece of bread . . . *Proverbs 6:26*

. . . many strong men have been slain by her.
Proverbs 7:26

they give gifts to all whores. . . . *Ezekiel 16:33*

RELIGION

THE MONOTHEISM of the Hebrew tribes is based in the belief that there is only one God, who is worshipped as the righteous ruler of the world, who dispenses justice, and is the giver of the law. His power results from his being the creator, who directs his creatures in ethical responsibility and high moral consciousness.

In Hebrew and Christian thought, religion is man's recognition of his relation to God and his expression of that relation in faith, worship, and conduct. It must be thought of as embodying the means of attaining and expressing in conduct the values deemed characteristic of the ideal life.

Babylon greatly influenced and molded Hebrew life and religion. This impact of Babylon commenced when Abraham began his journey to Canaan from the City of Ur in Babylon, carrying with him the language and culture which influenced future Hebrew life, and again when the place of captivity of Judah was in Babylon. This long captivity exerted formative influences upon the thought and worship of the Hebrews.

The law of God against "graven images" was so firm in the thinking of the Hebrews that graven images were not permitted to be brought into Jerusalem; not even Roman standards, with their eagles, were permitted during the days of the Roman occupation. Condemnation by God and by him through his prophets held the Hebrews close to the stanchion of Monotheism.

The prophet in Israel did not claim to speak from human wisdom. He claimed knowledge which ordinary man could not possess, representing divine inspiration and direct instruction by God as a result of which he unveiled and foretold the course of human events. He expressed the pleasure or displeasure of God, and in his foresight discerned more than the future; declaring what man could hope for or must fear in the eyes of God.

The content of the prophets divine communication was not exclusively foretelling the future, but was often accompanied by instruction concerning actions to be performed by the Hebrews in their conduct toward God.

When the prophecy was one of doom, predictions of the future were accompanied by instruction to follow the way of God.

The Bible warns against false prophets, but does not direct how man can determine who is a true prophet and who an imposter. Jesus warned: "Beware of false prophets, which come to you in sheep's clothing, but inwardly they are ravening wolves."

Great discussions have gone on for innumerable years about the day of the Sabbath. Originally, the sect of Hebrews who followed Christ, and who became known as Christians, observed the Sabbath in accordance with Mosaic law, as well as the first day of the week—Sunday —in respect of the resurrection, but there is no command in the New Testament in this regard.

Sunday was a pagan day sacred to the sun god and derives from the Mithraic religion. The resurrection having occurred on Sunday seemed sufficient reason for transferring the Sabbath to Sunday. Some time during the 4th Century, A.D., church law required this observance and

Emperor Constantine confirmed it by law. It is entirely possible that the early Christians, in observing the first rather than the seventh day, desired to distinguish themselves from the Hebrews and afford some public evidence that Christianity was not a new Hebrew sect.

An interesting court decision on observing the Sabbath is found in Tennessee, where the playing of professional baseball was declared not to be against the law prohibiting persons to do or exercise any of the common avocations of life on Sunday. The Supreme Court of that state ruled that since the law concerning Sunday was passed in 1803, and baseball as a game, was not played formally until 1845, there could not have been any intention on the part of the legislature to prohibit baseball, and therefore there was no violation of the statute. The decision makes no reference to the mandate in the Bible.

It is important to understand the background of the Gospels and the early expansion of Christianity, which was the only movement of any kind in ancient times which arose in the masses. Jesus, like his first followers, belonged to the poor. They listened to him, because he was one of them, and when Christianity spread into the Roman Empire its appeal was only to the poor.

The United States Supreme Court has said that the "establishment of religion" clause of the First Amendment, made equally applicable to the states by the Fourteenth Amendment, means that neither a state nor the Federal government can set up a church. Neither can pass laws which aid one religion, aid all religions, or prefer one religion over another. Neither can force or influence a person to go to or remain away from church against his will or force him to profess a belief or disbelief in any religion.

No person can be punished for entertaining or profess-ing religious beliefs or disbeliefs, or for church attend-ance or non-attendance. No tax in any amount, can be levied to support any religious activities or institutions, whatever they may be called, or whatever form they may adopt to teach or practice religion.

Neither a state nor the Federal government can, openly or secretly, participate in the affairs of any religious or-ganization or group, and vice versa.

In Biblical times it was just the opposite. The Bible was the law, and the law was the Bible. Belief was man-datory, and disbelief carried certain fixed penalties. Any violation of the Holy Scriptures was a sign against God, and secondly, a crime against the state. There was only one religion and all others were forbidden—"I am the Lord thy God . . . thou shalt have no other Gods before me."

THE BIBLICAL LAW

Blasphemy

And he that blasphemeth the name of the Lord, he shall surely be put to death. . . .   *Leviticus 24:16*

False Prophets

Beware of false prophets, which come to you in sheep's clothing, but inwardly they are ravening wolves.
Matthew 7:15

. . . Let not your prophets and your diviners . . . deceive you, neither harken to your dreams which ye cause to be dreamed. For they prophecy falsely unto you . . .
Jeremiah 29:8, 9

Holy Days

Six days shall work be done: but the seventh day is the sabbath of rest, an holy convocation; he shall do not work therein . . .
Leviticus 23:3

Three times thou shalt keep a feast unto me in the year. Thou shalt keep the feast of unleavened bread (passover) . . . and the feast of harvest, the first fruits of thy labors, which thou hast sown in the field: and the feast of ingathering, which is in the end of the year, when thou hast gathered thy labors out of the field.   *Exodus 23:14, 15, 16*

. . . abide ye every man in his place, let no man go out of his place on the seventh day.   *Exodus 16:29*

. . . bear no burden on the sabbath day, nor bring it in by the gates of Jerusalem; neither carry forth a burden out of your house on the sabbath, neither do ye any work . . .
Jeremiah 17:21, 22

Ye shall kindle no fire throughout your habitations upon the sabbath day. *Exodus 35:3*

And he (Jesus) came to Nazareth . . . and, as his custom was, he went into the synagogue on the sabbath day, and stood up for to read. *Luke 4:16*

Idolatry

Thou shalt not make unto thee any graven image . . . Thou shalt not bow down thyself to them, nor serve them. . . . *Exodus 20:4, 5*

For the devising of idols was the beginning of spiritual fornication, and the invention of them the corruption of life. *Wisdom of Solomon 14:12*

Turn yet not unto idols, nor make to yourselves molten gods . . . *Leviticus 19:4*

Thy graven images also will I cut off . . . and thou shalt no more worship the work of thine hands. *Micah 5:13*

Ye shall make you no idols nor graven image, neither rear you up a standing image, neither shall ye set up any image of stone in your land, to bow down to it . . . *Leviticus 26:1*

Priests

Fear the Lord . . . and reverence his priests . . . *Ecclesiasticus 7:29*

Fear the Lord and honor the priest; and give him his portion [of] the first fruits . . . *Ecclesiasticus 7:31*

And all the tithe of the land, whether of the seed of the land, or of the fruit of the tree, is the Lord's . . . *Leviticus 27:30*

And, behold, I have given the children of Levi all the tenth in Israel for an inheritance, for their service which they serve, even the service of the tabernacle of the congregation.

Numbers 18:21

We will not hearken to the king's words, to go from our religion, either on the right hand, or the left. *1 Maccabees 2:22*

And he [Christ] went into the temple, and began to cast out them that sold therein, and them that bought; Saying unto them, it is written, my house is the house of prayer: but ye have made it a den of thieves. *Luke 19:45, 46*

ROBBERY

IN ROBBERY under Biblical law, no penalty was imposed upon the offender who was required, however, to make restitution to the victim, and if he had nothing with which to make restitution "he shall be sold for his theft." The thief was sold into slavery by court order for as long as was necessary for him to make restitution, but in no event was the term to exceed six years.

This Biblical law was actually followed by the Hebrews. Zedekiah, King of Judah, ordered the princes and other wealthy persons to free their slaves, which they did, but seized the slaves again. As a result, the prophet Jeremiah, foretold the people that they would be delivered into the hands of their enemies to be destroyed.

In latter Biblical times, a thief could be sold into slavery only if he was unable to repay the actual value of the property stolen by him. If he repaid the actual amount, but was unable to pay the penalty of twofold, as imposed by the Biblical law, he could not be sold into slavery for the purpose of enabling him to pay that indemnity. Strangely enough, no woman could under any circumstances be sold into penal slavery.

THE BIBLICAL LAW

Thou shalt not defraud thy neighbor, neither rob him.
Leviticus 19:13

Rob not the poor. . . .   *Proverbs 22:22*

Whoso robbeth his father or his mother . . .. the same is the companion of a destroyer.   *Proverbs 28:24*

. . . This is the portion of them that spoil us, and the lot of them that rob us.   *Isaiah 17:14*

. . . and [they shall] rob those that robbed them . . .
Ezekiel 39:10

For they know not to do right, saith the Lord, who store up violence and robbery in their palaces.   *Amos 3:10*

. . . But ye say, wherein have we robbed thee?. . . .
Malachi 3:8

. . . and the robber swalloweth up their substance *Job 5:5*
As the partridge that broodeth over young which she hath not brought forth, so is he that getteth riches, and not by right; in the midst of his days he shall leave them, and at his end he shall be a fool.   *Jeremiah 17:11*

Then cried they all again, saying, not this man, but Barabbas. Now Barabbas was a robber.   *John 18:40*

. . . He that entereth not by the door . . . but climbeth up some other way, the same is a thief and a robber. *John 10:1*
Woe unto them that . . . rob the fatherless. *Isaiah 10:1, 2*

If a soul sin . . . he shall restore that which he took violently (by robbery) away. . . .   *Leviticus 6:2, 4*

SALES

Esau selling his birthright to Jacob is perhaps the first recorded sale in history of the right to inherit an estate. Potephar's buying of Joseph from the Ishmaelites in turn produced the first food administrator known to written history.

Biblical law prohibits dishonest sales of merchandise or the use of false weights and measures: "Thou shalt not have in thy bag divers weights, a great and a small. But thou shalt have a perfect and just weight, a perfect and just measure."

Sales of land "shall not be forever." This law preserved to each tribe the lands allotted them after the conquest of Canaan. There is no evidence of written documents of conveyance; the parties agreeing to the terms, the seller would give the buyer, before witnesses, some evidence or symbol of possession. The old English custom of "livery of seizin," or putting of a person in actual possession of land by performing some ceremony before witnesses which clearly placed the party in possession, was much the same as the Biblical manner of conveyance.

It appears that in later Biblical times, when writing came into usage, the methods of conveyance were much the same as in our law. When Jeremiah (32:9-14) purchased a field: "and I bought the field of Hanameel . . . and weighed him the money . . . and I subscribed the evidence and sealed it, and took witnesses . . . [and] I took the evidence of the purchase, both that which was sealed

. . . and that which was open: I gave the evidence unto Baruch . . in the sight of Hanameel and in the presence of witnesses that subscribed the book of the purchase, before all . . . that sat in the court . . . and I charged Baruch before them saying . . . take these evidences . . . both which is sealed . . . and this evidence which is open; and put them in an earthen vessel, that they may continue many days."

Under the law today the subject of sales is governed by statute.

THE BIBLICAL LAW

As a nail sticketh fast between the joinings of the stones; so doth sin stick close between buying and selling.

Ecclesiasticus 27:2

If thy brother be waxen poor, and hath sold away some of his possession, and if any of his kin come to redeem it, then shall he redeem that which his brother sold. *Leviticus 25:25*

The land shall not be sold forever: for the land is mine; for ye are strangers and sojourners with me. *Leviticus 25:23*

. . . in all land of your possession ye shall grant a redemption for the land. *Leviticus 25:24*

And I bought the field of Hanameel . . . and weighed him the money, even seventeen shekels of silver. And I subscribed the evidence (deed) and sealed it, and took witnesses, and weighed him the money in the balances. So I took the evidence of the purchase, both that which was sealed according to the law and custom . . . And I gave the evidence of the purchase unto Baruch . . . in the sight of Hanameel . . . and in the presence of the witnesses that subscribed the book of the purchase . . . and I charged Baruch before them saying . . . take these evidences . . . of the purchase, both which is sealed, and . . . which is open; and put them in an earthen vessel, that they may continue many days.

Jeremiah 32:9-14

He is a merchant, the balances of deceit are in his hand . . .

Hosea 12:7

. . . no devoted thing, that a man shall devote unto the Lord of all that he hath, both of man and beast, and of the field of his possession, shall be sold. . . .   *Leviticus 27:28*

. . . Thy money perish with thee, because thou hast thought that the gift of God may be purchased with money. *Acts 8:20*

If thou buy an Hebrew servant, six years he shall serve: and in the seventh he shall go out free for nothing. *Exodus 21:2*

And if a man sell his daughter to be a maidservant, she shall not go out as the menservants do.

If she please not her master . . . then shall he let her be redeemed.   *Exodus 21:7, 8*

He that withholdeth corn, the people shall curse him: but blessings shall be upon the head of him that selleth it.
                                                            Proverbs 11:26

And there was great famine in Samaria's and, behold . . . an ass's head was sold for fourscore pieces of silver and the fourth part of a cab of dove's dung for five pieces of silver.
                                                            2 Kings 6:25

. . . they were thy merchants: they traded the person of men and vessels of brass in thy market.   *Ezekiel 27:13*

Esau came from the field and he was faint. And Esau said to Jacob, feed me . . . for I am faint. And Jacob said swear to me this day; and he swore unto him: and he sold his birthright to Jacob. Then Jacob gave Esau bread and pottage of lentils.
                                                            Genesis 25:29, 34

Solomon had a vineyard . . . he let out the vineyard unto keepers; every one for the fruit thereof was to bring a thousand pieces of silver.   *Song of Solomon 8:11*

And if thou sell aught unto thy neighbor, or buyest aught of thy neighbor's hand, ye shall not oppress one another.
                                                            Leviticus 25:14

SURETY

MOST STATE LAWS define surety or guarantor as one who promises to answer for the debt, default, or miscarriage of another, or hypothecates property as security therefor. The obligation of a surety or guarantor arises only where there is a principal debtor. If there is no primary liability on the part of a third person, either express or implied, that is, if there is no debt, default or miscarriage, present or prospective, there is nothing to guarantee and there can be no contract of surety. Contracts of surety and contracts of guarantee were formerly separate and distinct matters but of late years they have been used as one synonymous term.

The laws of surety in the Bible are more than laws in the technical sense. They are philosophical directives pointing out the pitfalls when becoming surety, and at times justifying the act under specified conditions.

THE BIBLICAL LAW

And Judah said unto Israel his father, send the lad with me
. . . I will be surety for him; of my hand shalt thou require him:
if I bring him not unto thee, and set him before thee, let me
bear the blame forever. *Genesis 48:8, 9*

If he hath wronged thee, or oweth thee aught, put that on
mine account . . . I will repay it. *Philemon 18, 19*

. . . if thou be surety for thy friend . . . thou art snared with
the words of thy mouth. . . . *Proverbs 6:1, 2*

Be not one of them that . . . are sureties for debts.
Proverbs 22:26

Be not surety above thy power: for if thou be surety, take care
to pay it. *Ecclesiasticus 8:13*

Forget not the friendship of thy surety, for he has given his
life for thee: *Ecclesiasticus 29:15*

Suretyship hath undone many of good estate, and shaken them
as a wave of the sea: mighty men hath it driven from their
houses, so that they wandered among strange nations.
Ecclesiasticus 29:18

A man void of understanding striketh hands, and becometh
surety in the presence of his friends. *Proverbs 17:18*

An honest man is surety for his neighbor: but he that is impudent will forsake him. *Ecclesiasticus 29:14*

A sinner will overthrow the good estate of his surety: and he
that is of an unthankful mind will leave him [in danger] that
delivered him. *Ecclesiasticus 29:16, 17*

THEFT

AMONG THE Babylonians, larceny, under certain circumstances, was a crime punishable by death. Among the Athenians, and until a comparatively recent date in England, theft was a capital crime. Sir William Blackstone in his Commentaries, writes: "Our ancient Saxon laws nominally punished theft with death, if above the value of twelve pence; but the criminal was permitted to redeem his life by a pecuniary ransom; as, among their ancestors the Germans, by a stated number of cattle. But in the ninth year of Henry the First, this power of redemption was taken away, and all persons guilty of larceny above the value of twelve pence were directed to be hanged; which law continues in force to this day." Only as recently as the reign of George IV was capital punishment abolished for larceny in England.

Under the Biblical law, offenses committed against property were punishable only by a fine. In the case of larceny, the offender had to pay double the amount stolen: "If the theft be found in his possession alive, whether it be an ox, or ass, or a sheep, and kill it, he shall pay five oxen for an ox and four sheep for a sheep."

THE BIBLICAL LAW

Thou shalt not steal. *Exodus 20:15*

Whoso is partner with a thief hateth his own soul. . . .
Proverbs 29:24

. . . for everyone that stealeth shall be cut off. . . .
Zechariah 5:3

. . . it is not lawful to eat anything that is stolen. *Tobit 2:13*
Men do not despise a thief, if he steal to satisfy his soul when
he is hungry. *Proverbs 6:30*

Ye shall not steal, neither deal falsely. . . .
Leviticus 19:11

Then were there two thieves crucified with him . . .
Matthew 27:38

But if he [a thief] be found, he shall restore sevenfold . . .
Proverbs 6:31

If the theft be certainly found in his hand . . . he shall restore
double. *Exodus 22:4*

If a man shall steal an ox, or a sheep, and kill it or sell it; he
shall restore five oxen for an ox, and four sheep for a sheep.
Exodus 22:1

If a man shall deliver unto his neighbor money or stuff
to keep, and it be stolen out of the man's house; if the thief be
found, let him pay double. *Exodus 22:7*

. . . the day of the Lord so cometh as a thief in the night.
1 Thessalonians 5:2

TRESPASS

ANY UNLAWFUL interference with the property of another, or exercise of domain over it by which the owner is damnified is trespass. The basis of the offense is the injury to the complainant or to personal property in his possession.

In the common law trespass was limited to a direct invasion of property. In our law today, direct or indirect invasion of property is trespass, and may be committed by inconsequential and indirect injuries, as well as by direct and forcible injuries. The trespass must be intentional, or the result of recklessness or neglect, or the result of extra-hazardous activity.

Entry upon the lands of another, or into his house, may be a trespass. Entering a man's home without his permission, or the doing of any wilful act whether damaging or not is a violation of the law.

Trespass is an intentional harm, and for that reason there must be an intentional act done.

In the Bible a trespass is any transgression or offense against another. The trespass of today is a different offense than in Biblical days. Then trespass was committed if a man came "into the standing corn of thy neighbor, then thou mayest pluck the ears with thine hand; but thou shalt not move a sickle unto thy neighbor's standing corn."

In the early Biblical days one who felt he had been harmed sought vengeance on the cause of his harm, whether man or beast; often beasts such as cattle were killed because they injured a man or his property.

There is a form of trespass called malicious mischief by which another's property is damaged or destroyed. The Bible condemns all such acts, and cautions man not to trap his fellow but to be mindful of the danger of seeking another's downfall.

The Mosaic rule against unguarded excavations is the same as our law today. It provided then and it does now that it is negligence to leave open a pit wherein a person or animal may fall.

THE BIBLICAL LAW

For all manner of trespass, whether it be for ox, for ass, for sheep, for rainment, or for any manner of lost thing, which another challenges to be his, the cause of both parties shall come before the judges and whom the judges shall condemn, he shall pay double unto his neighbor. *Exodus 22:9*

Cursed be he that smiteth his neighbor secretly.
Deuteronomy 27:24

Lay hands suddenly on no man . . . *1 Timothy 6:22*

. . . if men strive together, and one smite another with a stone, or with his fist, and he die not, but keepeth his bed: if he rise again, and walk abroad upon his staff, then shall he that smote him be quit: only he shall pay for the loss of his time, and shall cause him to be thoroughly healed. *Exodus 21:18, 19*

If men strive and hurt a woman with child, so that her fruit depart from her, and yet no mischief follow; he shall . . . pay as the judges determine. *Exodus 21:22*

If fire break out, and catch in thorns, so that the stacks of corn, or the standing corn, or the field, be consumed therewith; he that kindled the fire shall surely make restitution. *Exodus 22:6*

Withdraw thy foot from thy neighbor's house lest he be weary of thee. . . , *Proverbs 25:17*

Remove not the old landmark; and enter not unto the fields of
the fatherless.   *Proverbs 23:10*

If a man shall cause a field or vineyard to be eaten, and shall
put in his beast, and shall feed in another man's field; of the
best of his own field, and of the best of his own vineyard, shall
he make restitution.   *Exodus 22:5*

When thou comest into thy neighbor's vineyard, then thou
mayest eat grapes thy fill at thine own pleasure; but thou shalt
not put any in thy vessel. When thou comest into the standing
corn of thy neighbor, then thou mayest pluck the ears with thine
hand; but thou shalt not move a sickle unto thy neighbor's standing corn.   *Deuteronomy 23:24, 25*

Wicked man . . .. deviseth mischief continually.
                                             Proverbs 6:12, 14

Thou shalt not . . . put a stumbling block before the blind . . .
                                             Leviticus 19:14

And if a man shall open a pit, or . . . dig a pit, and not cover
it, and an ox or an ass fall therein, the owner of the pit shall
make it good.   *Exodus 21:33, 34*

Woe to them that . . . take [fields] by violence . . .
                                             Micah 22:1, 2

. . . forgive, I pray thee now, the trespass of thy brethren.
                                             Genesis 50:17

. . . he shall recompense his trespass with the principal thereof,
and add unto it the fifth part thereof . . .   *Numbers 5:7*

. . . we have wronged no man, we have corrupted no man, we
have defrauded no man.   *2 Corinthians 7:2*

The wicked . . . deviseth mischief upon his bed . . .
                                             Psalms 36:1, 4

. . . a wicked man . . . deviseth mischief continually . . .
                                             Proverbs 6:12, 14

Whoso diggeth a pit shall fall therein: and he that setteth a
trap shall be taken therein.   *Ecclesiasticus 27:26*

WEIGHTS, MEASURES,
TIME, AND MONEY

THE BIBLICAL DAY was reckoned from evening to evening (Leviticus 23:32), a custom arising from the use of the Lunar months. The day was divided into morning, noon and evening.

Later, time was indicated by hours, the day consisting of twelve hours from sunrise to sunset, while the night was divided into three watches, the first, from sunset to midnight, the second, from midnight to cock-crow, the third from cock-crow to sunrise. The Romans divided the night into four watches.

The week consisted of seven days which were numbered with the exception of the seventh which was named the Sabbath.

The month was lunar (Genesis 1:14), as seen from the observance of the day of the new moon by special offerings to the Lord (Numbers 10:10), the Passover season coinciding with the full moon.

The year began in the spring with the month Abib that answered to a part of our March and April. This was the sacred year, and the annual festivals were directly related to the agricultural seasons. Thus Pentecost or Feast of Weeks occurred in Sivan (May-June), the feast of Ingathering, first-fruits of wine and oil, in Ethanim (September-October).

There was also a civil year beginning in the autumn with the month of Ethanim, hence the Jewish civil New Year's day in the fall and the commemoration of the Feast of Trumpets, Day of Atonement, Feast of Tabernacles. It was useful for a people devoted to agriculture to commence the year with the season of ploughing and sowing, and to close it with the harvest.

Our knowledge of Biblical weights and measure is incomplete and authorities differ as to values and quantities. Gold and silver were used as standards of value, and weights were estimated according to the number of grains of barley, taken from the middle of the ear, to which they were equivalent.

In the Old Testament, shekels, mina, talent, etc., signify a certain weight of metal. After the captivity it was Simon Maccabees (about 139 B.C.) who minted the first Hebrew coins. These consisted of copper, silver, gold, and later foreign coins, Greek Persian and Roman were in use in the Holy Land.

The chief unit was the shekel—weight. This was the principal weight by which others were regulated, and was subdivided into the bekah, half shekel, or half weight. The talent, or kikkar, was the largest weight for metals used by the Hebrews, both of gold and silver.

The purchasing power of money in Biblical times was probably more than a hundred and fifty times as great as at present. A Roman penny (about 17 cents) was considered fair compensation for a day's labor. Authorities have computed that the gift of the Queen of Sheba to King Solomon amounted to over one million dollars, while Judas received thirty pieces of silver ($17.00) for the betrayal of Jesus.

The hand was used for determining measurements—finger, palm, span and forearm. The smallest measure among the Hebrews was the breadth of the human finger. The palm or handbreadth was the breadth of four fingers —from three to three and a half inches. The span signifies the distance from the point of the thumb to the point of the little finger when stretched as far as possible. The cubit was the distance from the elbow to the end of the middle finger—about eighteen inches. The measuring reed was the "sweet cane (Ezekiel 40:3, 5; 42:15, 16) ." It was equal to six cubits, or about nine and a half to ten feet. Reference to these measuring methods is also to be found in Genesis 6, Exodus 25 and Acts 27.

Dry measure was divided into cab, omer, seah and ephah. The word cab occurs only in II Kings 6:25, and the word omer only in Exodus 16:16-36, while ephah of Egyptian origin occurs frequently and in capacity was equivalent to the liquid measure—bath. The cab was a little more than a quart, and the omer two quarts. The ephah equalled about three pecks.

In liquid measure the log is the smallest of the biblical series. Log originally meant a basin. The word hin, of Egyptian origin is the equal of twelve logs. The word bath is first mentioned in I Kings 7:26 and is the largest of the liquid measures. In quantity it is equal to the Ephah. The log was about two-thirds of a pint, and the bath about five gallons.

THE BIBLICAL LAW

Divers weights, and divers measures, both of them are alike abomination to the Lord. *Proverbs 20:10*

. . . the scant measure . . . is abominable. Shall I count them pure with the wicked balances, and with the bag of deceitful weights? *Micah 6:10, 11*

A false balance is abomination to the Lord; but a just weight is his delight. *Proverbs 11:1*

Ye shall do no unrighteousness in judgment, in meteyard, in weight, or in measure. Just balances [and] just weights shall ye have. *Leviticus 19:35, 36*

Of these things be not thou ashamed . . . of exactness of balances and weights. *Ecclesiasticus 42:1, 4*

Thou shalt not have in thy bag divers weights, a great and a small. But thou shalt have a perfect and just weight, a perfect and just measure shalt thou have. *Deuteronomy 25:13, 15*
. . . with what measure ye mete, it shall be measured to you again. *Matthew 7:2*

. . . Thou art weighed in the balances, and art found wanting. *Daniel 5:27*

WILLS

A WILL is an instrument for the disposition of one's property to take effect after death. It is the declaration of a man's intentions which he wills to be performed after his death concerning the disposition of his property, and the manner of handling such other matters as he may direct.

There is nothing which so generally strikes the imagination as the sole and despotic dominion which one man claims and exercises over the external things of the world, in total exclusion of the right of any other individual.

However, the most effectual way of abandoning property is by the death of the owner, when both the actual possession and intention of keeping possession ceasing, the property which is founded upon such possession and intention ought also to cease. But as governments are calculated for the peace of mankind, it is the universal law of almost every nation to give the dying person a power of continuing his property by disposing of his possessions by will.

Biblical law provides that the property possessed by man at the time of death should pass to his son or sons to the exclusion of daughters. In early American law, property was equally divided among the children; both sons and daughters.

The rules of succession are not overlooked in the law of Moses. Even as today, the succession follows rules which cannot be waived or altered.

There are Biblical deviations from the fixed rules. In one instance, a man left five daughters and no son, and the daughters petitioned Moses that their father's property be awarded to them. This Moses granted on the ground that the name of their father would otherwise be done away with (Numbers 27:4). Thereafter, the Elders of Gilead sought a ruling as to what should be done on the marriage of the five daughters so as to prevent their inheritance from passing to another tribe. Moses then ruled that the daughters could marry whomever they thought best, but such marriage must be only to the family of the tribe of their fathers (Numbers 36:6, 7, 8 and 9).

In Biblical times there was no knowledge or use of wills as we understand them today. Each person who had property would give it to the heirs before death whenever possible; otherwise, it descended according to the Mosaic laws of succession.

The oldest written will of which we have any knowledge was made in Egypt about 2,500 years B.C. There is no evidence of any written wills being used in Israel. Because each tribe controlled the assets of all its members, there was no necessity for documents of conveyance or inheritance.

THE BIBLICAL LAW

... where a testament is, there must also of necessity be the death of the testator. For a testament is of force after men are dead: otherwise it is of no strength at all while the testator liveth.
Hebrews 9:16, 17

Is it now lawful for me to do what I will with mine own?
Matthew 20:15

... set thine house in order: for thou shalt die. . . .
Isaiah 38:1

A good man leaveth an inheritance . . .   *Proverbs 33:22*

... If a man die, and have no son then ye shall cause his inheritance to pass unto his daughter. And if he have no daughter, then ye shall give his inheritance unto his brethren. And if he have no brethren, then ye shall give his inheritance unto his father's brethren. And if his father have no brethren, then ye shall give his inheritance unto his kinsman that is next to him of his family, and he shall possess it. . . . *Numbers 27:8, 9, 10, 11*

And every daughter, that possesseth an inheritance in any tribe of the children of Israel, shall be wife unto one of the family of the tribe of her father, that the children of Israel may enjoy every man the inheritance of his father. Neither shall the inheritance remove from one tribe to another tribe; but every one of the tribes of the children of Israel shall keep himself to his own inheritance.   *Numbers 36:8, 9*

A good man leaveth an inheritance to his children's children.
Proverbs 13:22

... but he that shall come forth out of thine own bowels shall be thine heir.   *Genesis 15:4*

Thou shalt not inherit in our father's house; for thou art the son of a strange woman.   *Judges 11:2*

At the time when thou shalt end thy days, and finish thy life, distribute thine inheritance.   *Ecclesiasticus 33:23*

WOMAN

In a generic sense the word woman means the female part of the human race. In Biblical times women had little or no equality with man. She was under his supervision and control and from birth was taught her secondary position in the scheme of life. She could not own property nor could she inherit except by special dispensation of the tribal head, or as in Mosaic days, by special decree of Moses.

The word woman comes from the English Saxon word, wiman in the Saxon, i.e. wife, and sometimes it is by the Saxons derived from wamb, or wombe-man.

The Bible has a different reason for calling the female woman. As written in Genesis 2: "And the Lord caused a deep sleep to fall upon Adam and he slept: and he took one of his ribs and closed up the flesh instead thereof; and the rib which the Lord God had taken from man, made he a woman, and brought her into the man. And Adam said, This is now bone of my bones, and flesh of my flesh: she shall be called Woman, because she was taken out of man."

As late as the New Testament, St. Paul said: "Let your women keep silence in the churches; for it is not permitted unto them to speak; but they are commanded to be under obedience. . . ."

Hundreds of years would pass until woman would be recognized as man's equal. Wars and the economy of the world brought about the equality of the sexes, but at an awful price. The calm reserve of woman has been displaced by the anxiety of equal opportunity, and the respectful seclusion of the female sex has been displaced by the hardness of competitive existence.

In the history of the Hebrew people there have been but two women who governed their country: Jezebel's daughter Athalia who ruled Judea from 842 to 836 B.C., and Queen Salome Alexandra, who succeeded to the throne after the death of her husband in 76 B.C.

THE BIBLICAL LAW

Forego not a wise and good woman: for her grace is above gold.   *Ecclesiasticus 7:19*

. . . that women adorn themselves in modest apparel, with shamefacedness and sobriety; not with braided hair, or gold, or pearls, or costly array; but (which becometh women professing godliness) with good works.   *1 Timothy 2:9, 10*

Let women learn in silence with all subjection.
1 Timothy 2:11

. . . let it not be that outward adorning of plaiting the hair, and of wearing of gold, or of putting on of apparel; but let be the hidden man of the heart . . . For after this manner in the old time the holy women also, who trusted in God, adorned themselves, being in subjection unto their own husbands.
1 Peter 3:3, 4, 5

But I suffer not a woman to teach, nor to usurp authority over the man, but to be in silence.   *1 Timothy 2:12*
Let your women keep silence in the churches; for it is not permitted unto them to speak; but they are commanded to be under obedience . . .   *1 Corinthians 14:34*

And if they [women] will learn anything, let them ask their husbands at home: for it is a shame for women to speak in the church.   *1 Corinthians 14:35*

The aged women likewise, that they be in behavior as becomes holiness, nor false accusers, not given to much wine, teachers of

good things; that they may teach the young women to be sober, to love their husbands, to love their children, to be discreet, chaste, keepers at home, good, obedient to their own husbands . . .
Titus 2:2, 3, 4, 5

All wickedness is but little to the wickedness of a women . . .
Ecclesiasticus 25:19

As a jewel of gold in a swine's snout, so is a fair woman which is without discretion. *Proverbs 11:22*

An evil wife is a yoke shaken to and fro: he that hath hold of her is as though he held a scorpion. *Ecclesiasticus 26:7*

A drunken woman and a gadder abroad causeth great anger, and she will not cover her own shame. *Ecclesiasticus 26:8*

Give the water no passage; neither a wicked woman liberty to gad abroad. *Ecclesiasticus 25:25*

Thou shalt not approach unto a woman to uncover her nakedness, as long as she is put aside for her uncleanness (menstruation). *Leviticus 18:19*

And if a man shall lie with a woman having her sickness . . . both of them shall be cut off from among their people. *Leviticus 20:18*

The woman also with whom man shall lie with seed of copulation, they shall both bathe themselves in water, and be unclean until the even. *Leviticus 15:18*

The woman shall not wear that which pertaineth unto man. . . . *Deuteronomy 22:5*

The tender and delicate woman among you, which would not adventure to set the sole of her foot upon the ground for delicateness and tenderness, her eye shall be evil toward the husband of her bosom, and toward her son, and toward her daughter. *Deuteronomy 28:56*

I will therefore that the younger women marry, bear children, guide the house, give none occasion to the adversary to speak reproachfully. *1 Timothy 5:14*

The whoredom of a woman may be known in her haughty looks and eyelids. *Ecclesiasticus 26:9*